American Bald Eagles in Intarsia

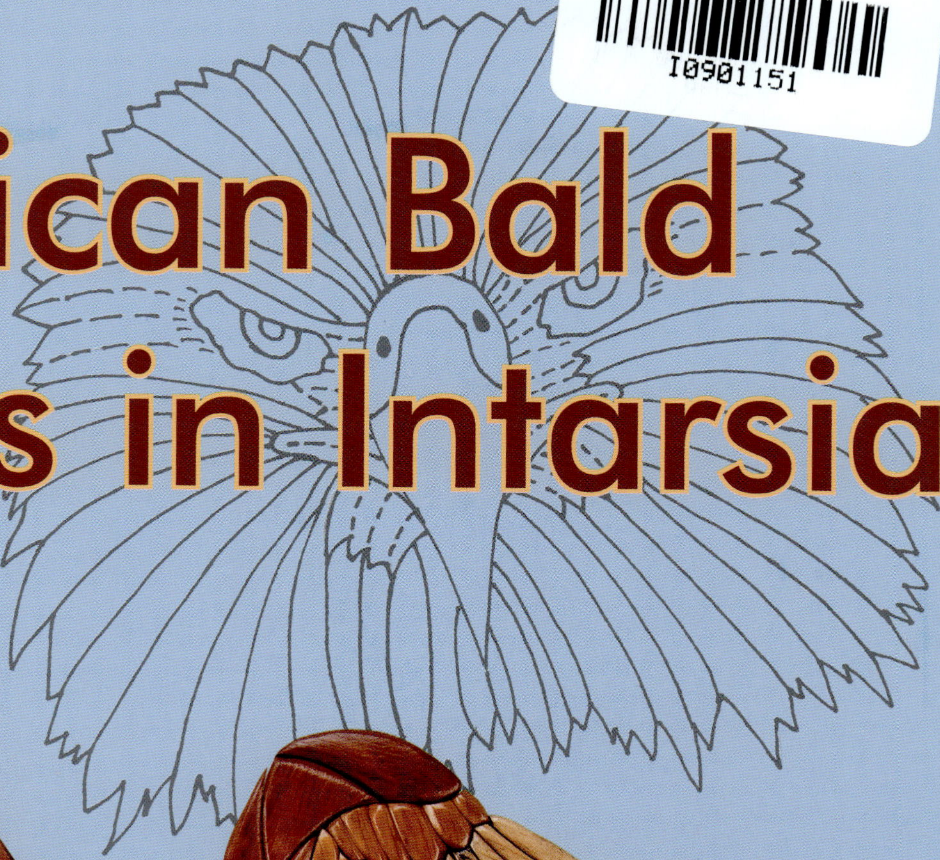

Volume 1: Patriotic

Schiffer Publishing Ltd
4880 Lower Valley Road • Atglen, PA 19310

Ralph S. Buckland

Ralph and his wife, Kathy, with Chester.

This book is dedicated to Kathy, my wife.

A special thanks to my daughter-in-law, Dinah Thornton-Buckland; photographer, Bruce M. Waters for photographs of the finished eagle projects; designer, Mark Bowyer; and my editor, Jesse Marth.

Other Schiffer Books By The Author:

Turning Segmented Lamps, 978-0-7643-3795-6, $29.99

Other Schiffer Books on Related Subjects:

Lighted Scroll Saw Projects, 978-0-7643-3386-6, $24.99

The Artistic Scrollsaw: Wonders of Nature, 978-0-7643-2676-9, $12.95

Library of Congress Control Number: 2012931897

Designed by Mark David Bowyer
Type set in Future Lt BT / Minion Pro

ISBN: 978-0-7643-4113-7
Printed in China

Schiffer Books are available at special discounts for bulk purchases for sales promotions or premiums. Special editions, including personalized covers, corporate imprints, and excerpts can be created in large quantities for special needs. For more information contact the publisher:

Published by Schiffer Publishing Ltd.
4880 Lower Valley Road
Atglen, PA 19310
Phone: (610) 593-1777; Fax: (610) 593-2002
E-mail: Info@schifferbooks.com

For the largest selection of fine reference books on this and related subjects, please visit our website at
www.schifferbooks.com
We are always looking for people to write books on new and related subjects. If you have an idea for a book, please contact us at
proposals@schifferbooks.com

This book may be purchased from the publisher.
Please try your bookstore first.
You may write for a free catalog.

In Europe, Schiffer books are distributed by
Bushwood Books
6 Marksbury Ave.
Kew Gardens
Surrey TW9 4JF England
Phone: 44 (0) 20 8392 8585; Fax: 44 (0) 20 8392 9876
E-mail: info@bushwoodbooks.co.uk
Website: www.bushwoodbooks.co.uk

Contents

Preface 4

Chapter I: An Introduction and History of Intarsia 5

Chapter II: Topic Section: Processes and Techniques 6

Chapter III: Easy Eagle 20

Chapter IV: Twenty-Four Inch Eagle 31

Chapter V: The Stern Eagle 53

Chapter VI: Born Free Eagle 60

Chapter VII: The Great Seal of the United States of America 74

Preface

Intarsia artists, today, use woods of different colors and textures to create pictorial designs. Projects in this book use a variety of domestic and exotic woods.

America Bald Eagles in Intarsia, Volume I is divided into seven chapters. Chapter I deals with the history of intarsia. Chapter II explains in detail techniques and processes common to projects in the book. Chapter III through chapter VII provide detailed instructions and patterns for each eagle. Starting with Chapter III, "Easy Eagle One," the eagle projects progress from very simple (5 pieces and an easy eye and backer board) to eagles having approximately 100 pieces, ideal for the intermediate to advanced woodworker.

Throughout the book you will find safety tips. Before attempting any woodworking be sure you read, understand, and follow manufacturer's safety guidelines. This should always be a woodworker's first priority. I also encourage you to read through this book completely before you start working to better familiarize yourself with the techniques and process. Finally, I hope creating eagle intarsia plaques will be inspirational and personally rewarding to you.

Chapter I

An Introduction and History of Intarsia

The ancient art form of intarsia involves cutting and fitting pieces of wood together to form a design or a picture. Other materials were used early in the history of intarsia such as stone, mother-of-pearl, and ivory. Often hundreds or even thousands of pieces may be assembled to create a design. This art form dates back as far as the early Egyptian civilization. The word "intarsia" comes from the Latin verb which means to insert. Intarsia, unlike inlay, usually uses pieces from 1/4" to 2" thick. The edges of an intarsia project are often rounded to add depth to the art form. Artisans today use natural colors of wood instead of using stain. In this book, I used stain only on a few parts for the project in the last chapter, "The Great Seal of the United State of America."

The American bald eagle was used for the Great Seal of the United States of America in June 1782. Generally, it was recognized as the national bird but at that time it was not official. Benjamin Franklin, in 1784, expressed a strong disapproval for the eagle being the national bird. He thought the eagle had a bad moral character and was somewhat of a scavenger. Franklin wanted the turkey to become the national bird because it was native to America and he thought a more respectable bird. Personally, I'm glad we adopted the eagle instead of the turkey. I would have found it hard to write a woodworking book about turkeys.

In 1789, the American eagle became the official national bird during George Washington's presidency. In 1940, the American bald eagle was protected by the National Emblem Act.

Today, the bald eagle can be found all over North America. Many live along America's Pacific Coast and flourish in Canada and Alaska. But they can be found in many states, from our border with Mexico and along the Atlantic Coast, especially in the northern areas of New England, Nova Scotia, Newfoundland, and Labrador.

Eagles are a very powerful bird and they have a wing span up to eight feet. They weigh up to fourteen pounds. Their nest have been found to be as large as ten feet in diameter.

Now, step by step, I invite you to capture the majesty of this great American symbol using the ancient art of intarsia.

Chapter II

Topic Section: Processes and Techniques

This chapter describes in detail the processes, techniques, and woods as well as some resources that are used to create the eagles throughout the book. Included is a list of woods used.

But first, here is a list of all the necessary tools and materials used to make these intarsia eagle projects:

Tools & Materials

CA glue
Disc sander
Drill press
Drum sander
Electric hand drill
Forstner bit
InLace® (see "Resources for Materials")
Kreg® screws and pocket system
Lathe, lathe faceplate, and basic lathe tools
Manila paper folders
Orbital sander
Picture hangers
Power miter box
Radial arm saw
Sand-O-Flex® sander
Stain (for the Great Seal project)
Table saw
Table scroll saw (jig saw)
Titebond® glue
Variety of basic woodworking hand tools
Woodburner

I. Methods for Making the Eagle Eye

Plug Cutter Method: This is one of the easiest methods for making an eye. In this example I use yellow heart wood. Notice that I am making four plugs *(Fig. 2-1)*. Even though I only need one, it is a good idea to make a few extra and then pick the best.

Next, drill a hole in the center for the pupil *(Fig. 2-2)* and make some plugs for the pupil; coco bolo is used here *(Fig. 2-3)*. These can be easily removed by wedging them out with a screwdriver *(Figs. 2-4 & 2-5)*.

Glue the dark plug in the hole for the pupil *(Fig. 2-6)*. When it is dry, sand and smooth using a disc sander *(Figs. 2-7 & 2-8)*.

Fig. 2-1: Making a few extra plugs.

Fig. 2-2: Using a twist bit for drilling holes for the pupils.

Fig. 2-3: Making pupils using a plug cutter.

Fig. 2-6: Gluing the plug into the hole.

Fig. 2-4: Insert a screwdriver on the edge of the plug.

Fig. 2-7: Sanding the eye flat on a belt sander.

Fig. 2-5: Prying the plug out.

Fig. 2-8: Three good eyes.

Draw a line on the top of the wood *(Fig. 2-9)* and use a band saw to cut them out *(Fig. 2-10)*. Notice I've used a block of wood so the eyes don't fall through the throat of the band saw and get lost.

In some cases you may only want 3/4 of an eye; the other 1/4 can be easily sanded using a pair of pliers and a disc sander *(Figs. 2-11 & 2-12)*.

Fig. 2-9: The guideline for the band saw on the top of the wood.

Fig. 2-10: Using a band saw, cut along the pencil line. The eye will pop out as you cut. Notice the board used to catch the eyes so they don't fall through the throat of the band saw.

Fig. 2-11: Sanding the eye flat on one side as would be needed for 3/4 of an eye.

Fig. 2-12: The flattened, 3/4 eye glued into place.

InLace Method: This method starts in the same manner as the plug cutter method. Make the plug, and drill the hole the size that you need. Using the manufacturer's instruction for InLace, fill the pupil *(Fig. 2-13)*. Once this is dry use a disc sander to sand these smooth. Remove the excess InLace with a plug cutter *(Fig. 2-14)*. Then use the same method to remove the plugs as was described in the plug cutter method. The InLace method will also work well on Easy Eagle.

Fig. 2-13: InLace spread inside the pupil.

Fig. 2-14: Clearing out excess InLace with a plug cutter.

Jig Saw Method: This method is used for the Stern Eagle *(Fig. 2-15)*. Notice that all the feathers below the eye section are cut out individually. The eye fits into the cottonwood (the white wood*)* which is one piece. The two lines to the right of the eye are burnt with a woodburner; they are not cut.

To make the eye on the left side of the eagle, drill a hole where the eye section will go *(Fig. 2-16)*. Insert the jig saw blade through the hole and cut out the eye section *(Figs. 2-17 & 2-18)*.

Fig. 2-15: The Stern Eagle.

Fig. 2-16: Drilling the hole in the eye.

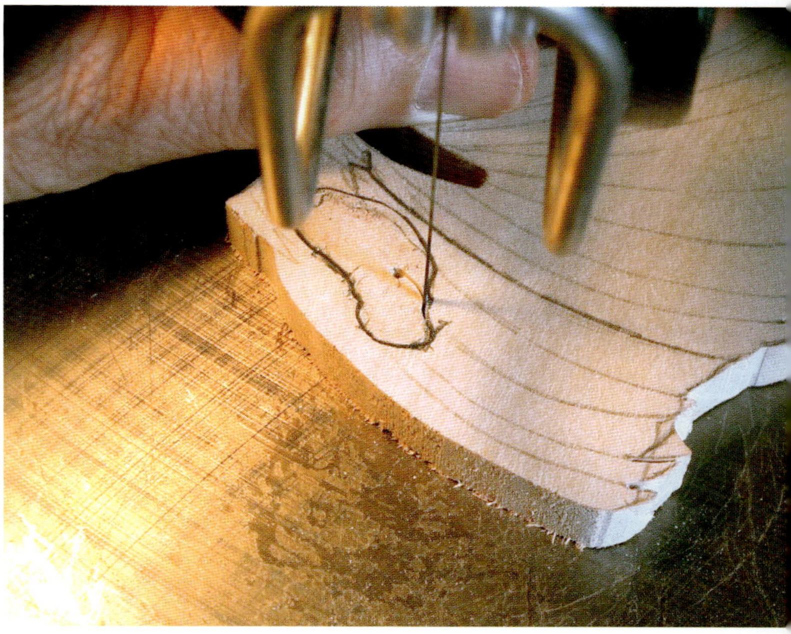

Fig. 2-17: Starting the internal cut.

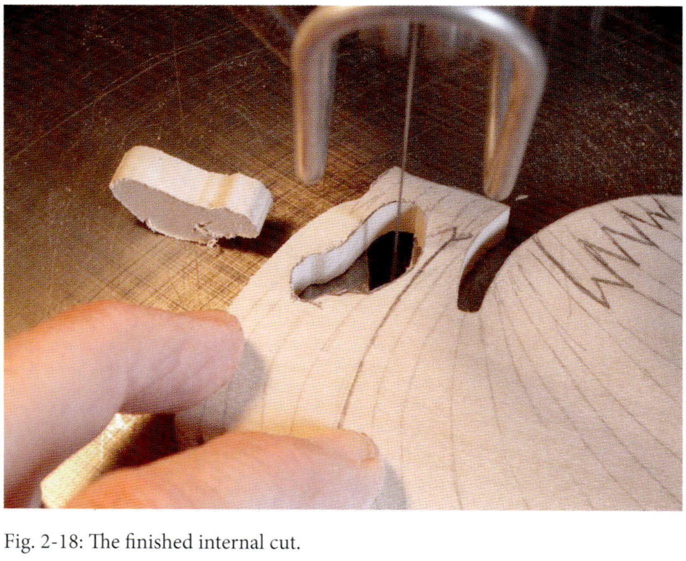

Fig. 2-18: The finished internal cut.

Using a scrap piece of yellow heart and a piece of double-sided tape, tape the yellow heart to a piece of wenge *(Fig. 2-19)*. These two pieces should be the same thickness as the white wood they fit into. That is, they fit into the eye section which you previously cut out. Using your jig saw, cut out the pupil *(Fig. 2-20)*. Then continue and cut out the rest of the eye section *(Fig. 2-21)*. Glue the wenge and the yellow heart together as shown in *Fig. 2-22*. The eye section should be sanded smooth on the front so it is about 1/16" to 1/8" less in thickness than the white cottonwood it will fit into *(Figs. 2-23 & 2-24)*.

Fig. 2-19: Wenge and yellow heart glued together temporarily.

Fig. 2-20: Cutting out the pupil.

Fig. 2-21: Cutting the remaining part of the eye.

Fig. 2-22: The eye with wenge and yellow heart glued together.

Fig. 2-23: Flattening the eye on the disc sander.

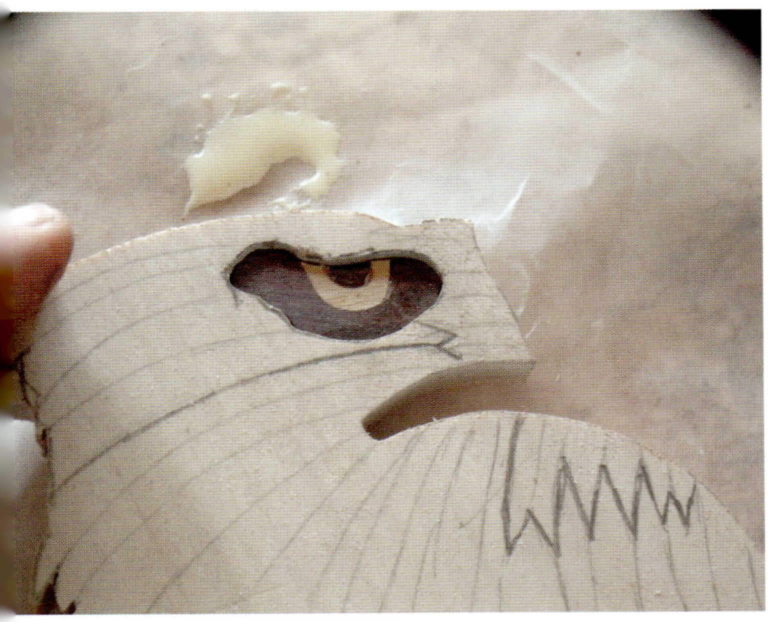

Fig. 2-24: The eye has been recessed.

II. Backer Boards

Several types of backer boards are used for displaying the eagles in this book. Easy Eagle I's backer board is made from purple heart with yellow heart sides glued on. In this case, additional plywood backer boards are not needed and you can attach your hanger directly to the purple heart. The photograph shows gluing the yellow heart sides to the purple heart *(Fig. 2-25)*.

On the Great Seal a backer board is not needed. Turn the cottonwood and the walnut edge *(Figs. 2-26 & 2-27)*. And again the hanger can be attached directly to the cottonwood.

When using a backer board, such as the plywood or lauan or even a solid piece of wood, the edge will appear white when viewed from the side. Use a dark permanent marker, black or brown, and color the edge. Sometimes I'll use a dark stain to stain the edges before I place the eagle on.

Fig. 2-25: The backer board is made of solid 3/4" purple heart and yellow heart; plywood not needed.

Fig. 2-26: Cutting a cove using a round-nosed tool.

Fig. 2-27: Sanding a backer board as it turns.

III. Hangers

There are a number of commercial hangers available. A saw-tooth hanger is easily driven into the plywood *(Fig. 2-28)*. For harder woods you may need to drill a small hole to drive the nail. Another method I use, particularly on the larger projects where you may have two hangers, is the screw and wire method *(Fig. 2-29)*. Simply wrap a wire around two screws. I like to leave the wire loose which allows me to bend it in such a way so I can look behind the project as I hang it *(Fig. 2-30)*. Looking behind the project with the saw-tooth method, it is difficult to see the hangers due to the lack of space. The wire method is easier to see because the wire can be bent to give you more space to see what you are doing. The hardware I use for the wall is shown in *Fig. 2-31*. There are several sizes available.

Fig. 2-30: Large intarsia projects may require two hangers.

Fig. 2-28: A saw-tooth shaped commercial hanger.

Fig. 2-29: Two screws and a wire make a great hanging device.

Fig. 2-31: A commercial hanging device driven into the drywall.

IV. Janka Scale

The Janka Scale is used to determine the hardness and/or the density of various types of wood. A steel ball is pressed into the face of the wood (never the end grain) and depending on the force necessary to bury the ball half-way into the wood will determine the hardness or density. Cutting some of the hardwoods used in this book on the jig saw will go very slowly and other woods, like cottonwood, will cut very easily. Listed below are most of the woods used in this book as well as their Janka rating.

Name of Wood	Janka Scale Hardness Rating
Lignum Vitae	4500
Black Ebony	3220
Bloodwood	2900
Brazilian Cherry/Jatoba	2350
Purpleheart	1860
Padauk	1725
Wenge	1630
Hard Maple	1450
American Birch	1300
Red Oak	1290
Coco Bolo	1136
Black Walnut	1010
Lace Wood	840
Sycamore	770

Balsa wood is the lowest wood listed on the Janka Scale with a rating of 100. This wood is not used on any of the eagles. The wood flooring industry uses the Janka Scale to determine the suitability of wood for floors.

V. Types of Woods Used

Lignum vitae is considered the world's hardest wood. I use it for its green color. It is sometimes referred to as green wood. The olives on the Great Seal are lignum vitae.

Black ebony is a very black wood with little grain pattern showing on the face of the wood. It is native to India and Africa. The claws on the Twenty-Four Inch Eagle are made from black ebony.

Bloodwood has a very deep red color. I used it on the Great Seal and the Stern Eagle. Bloodwood is found in South America.

Jatoba or Brazilian cherry has a similar color to American cherry. I used it on the Twenty-Four Inch Eagle. It grows in Central and South America.

Purpleheart is found in Central and South America. It is used for the background of Easy Eagle I. This wood has a very rich purple color.

Wenge is used where I need a dark colored wood. It is less expensive then black ebony. If you look at it very closely, you will see that it has black and brown colors. The Born Free Eagle uses wenge for the black feathers and the wings.

Hard maple is found in North America. A good example of hard maple are the feathers of Easy Eagle I.

Beech grows not only in North America but also Europe and Asia. Although I have not used beech in this book it would be a nice wood for the feathers of the eagles.

Red oak is plentiful in southern Canada and much of United States.

Black walnut grows especially well in the eastern part of the United States as well as other areas of the U.S. It is easily worked hard wood with a rich brown color. It is used throughout the book for the eagles' body and parts of the wings.

Sycamore is plentiful in North America and has a creamy white color.

Cottonwood is used throughout the book on many of the eagles. It has a pure white color and is ideal for the eagle's head and tail feathers. Cottonwood is a very soft wood and easily cut.

Spalted maple has black lines and is often discolored. This is caused by fungus growing in the tree or log. Spalted maple is used for the mountain on the Born Free Eagle.

VI. Resources for Materials

Listed below are some of the sources for materials used in this book.

Material	Websites
Scroll Saw Blades	www.rockler.com
	www.olsonsaw.com
	www.sloanswoodshop.com
InLace	www.woodturnerscatalog.com
	www.turtlefeathers.net
Stars (Colorbok Mini Brad)	www.joann.com
CA Glue	www.rockler.com
	www.woodturnerscatalog.com
Sand-O-Flex	www.meritindustries.com
	www.industrialabrasives.com
Hangers	www.craftparts.com
	www.woodwerks.com

VII. Tracing Patterns or Objects

When tracing one pattern on top of another, an example would be the eye of the Stern Eagle, use the process shown in *Fig. 2-32*. Trace around the outside of the object as shown in Detail A. Notice in Detail B that the saw blade and the cut is on the inside of the pencil mark. Detail C shows placing the part you just traced into the part that you have just cut out. Notice that you leave the pencil line.

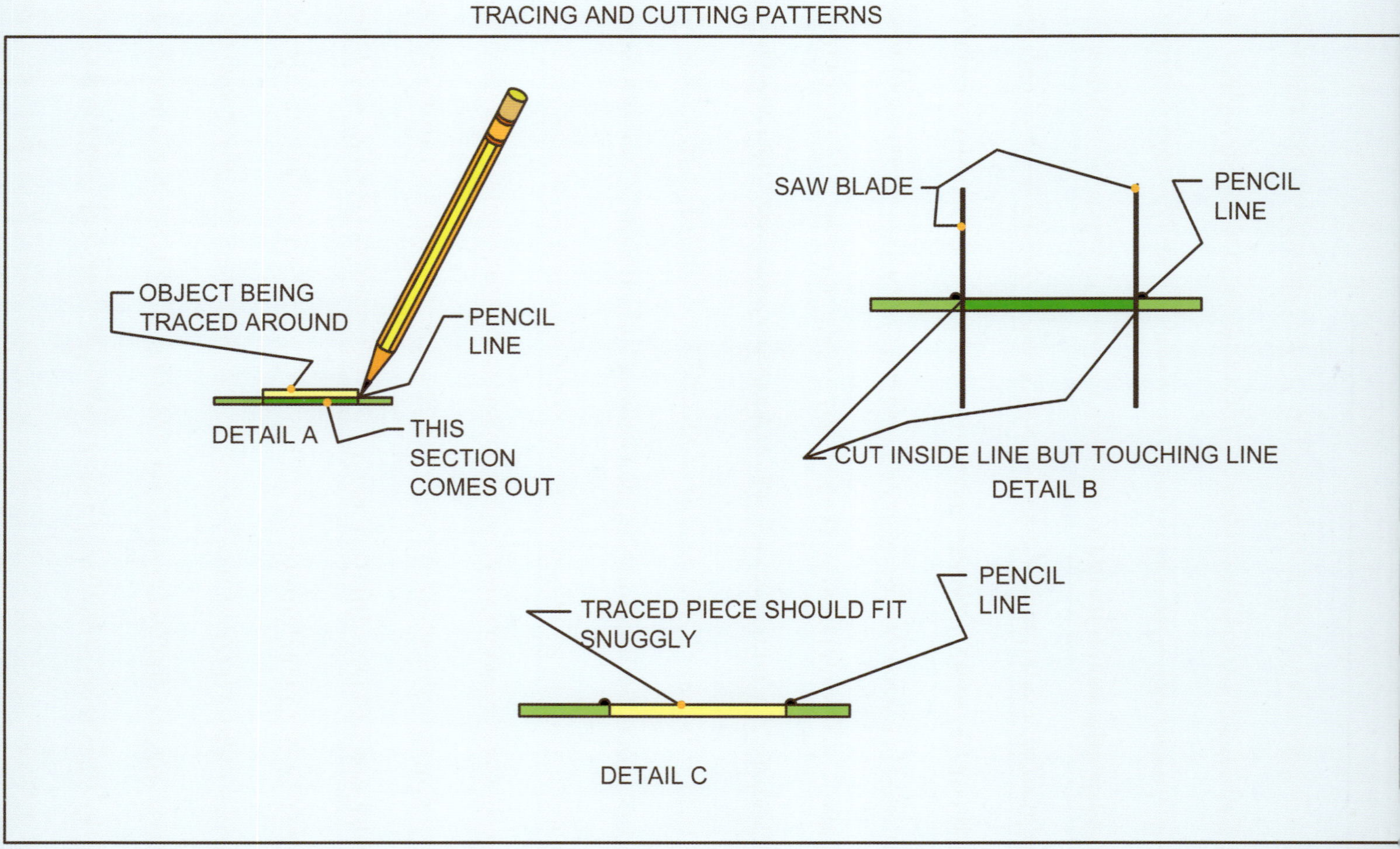

Fig. 2-32

VIII. Segmented Turning

The circular frame on the The Great Seal uses a process called segmented turning. Normally, when you turn a piece of wood it would be in one piece. An example, would be a baseball bat. This process of turning between two centers or two points is called spindle turning. Another method is called faceplate turning. Usually, woodturners would turn a solid piece of wood attached to a cast iron disc which screws to the lathe. As the piece turns they can recreate various shapes. This faceplate process is used predominately in segmented turning.

In both of the processes mentioned above, faceplate and spindle turning, usually the project will have one or several pieces of wood glued together. Segmented turning is done by constructing rings (see Detail A in *Fig. 2-33).* These rings commonly have four, eight, or sixteen parts called segments, although they can have any number of segments that are multiples of 360 degrees. The rings are glued together on top of each other. By using different colored segments and arranging them in various patterns, an infinite number of designs can be made. Detail B and C *(Fig. 2-33)* show how a piece created with segmented turning might be constructed.

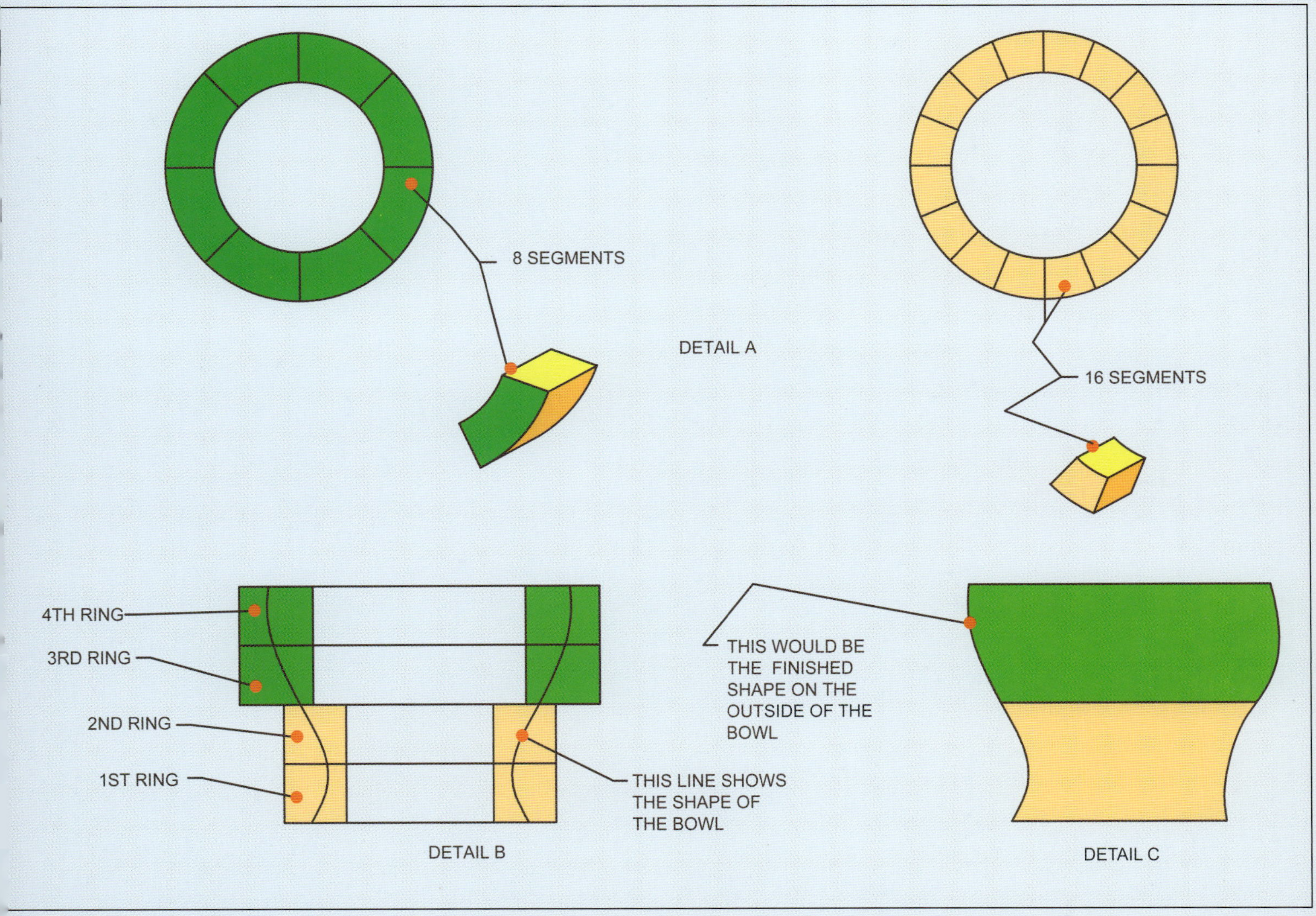

Figure 2-34 shows a lamp made by using the segmented turning process. It would not be unusual for a segmented project to have 20, 30, or more rings or layers. These rings can have hundreds or even thousands of segments arranged in interesting and unique designs.

Fig. 2-34:
A segmented lamp made from yellow heart and blood wood. Plans for this lamp and other segmented lamps are in the author's book, *Turning Segmented Lamps*, Schiffer Publishing, Ltd.

IX. Undercutting

Undercutting is a process which can help create a better fit for intarsia parts. The drawing *(Fig. 2-35)* shows two pieces of wood that have a poor fit. There is a gap between the pieces. This often occurs when you have a curved piece and the two curves do not match correctly. Notice the undercut in the drawing, which is an angular cut, allows the top to fit well but not the bottom. The top is the part that will show on your project and give the appearance of a perfect fit and the bottom will not. The fit at the bottom does not matter because it will not show on the project.

X. Internal Cut

The internal cut is an inside cut and is usually done on a jig or scroll saw *(Fig. 2-36)*. Step 1 shows the section of a project the needs to be cut out. In step 2, a hole is drilled and the blade is inserted through the hole. Put the blade in the top chuck and then your bottom chuck on your jig saw. Then, on the pattern shown, you will want to make two cuts. Step 3 shows the section that has been cut out. Step 4 shows the finished internal cut. At this point you can take the blade out of the upper and lower chuck and remove the piece of wood which now has an internal cut.

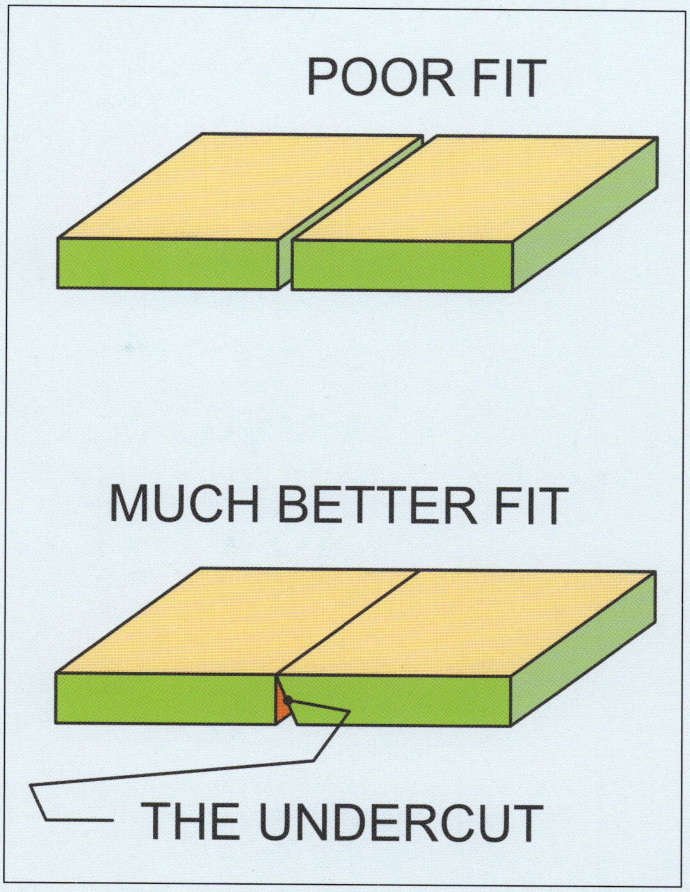

Fig. 2-35

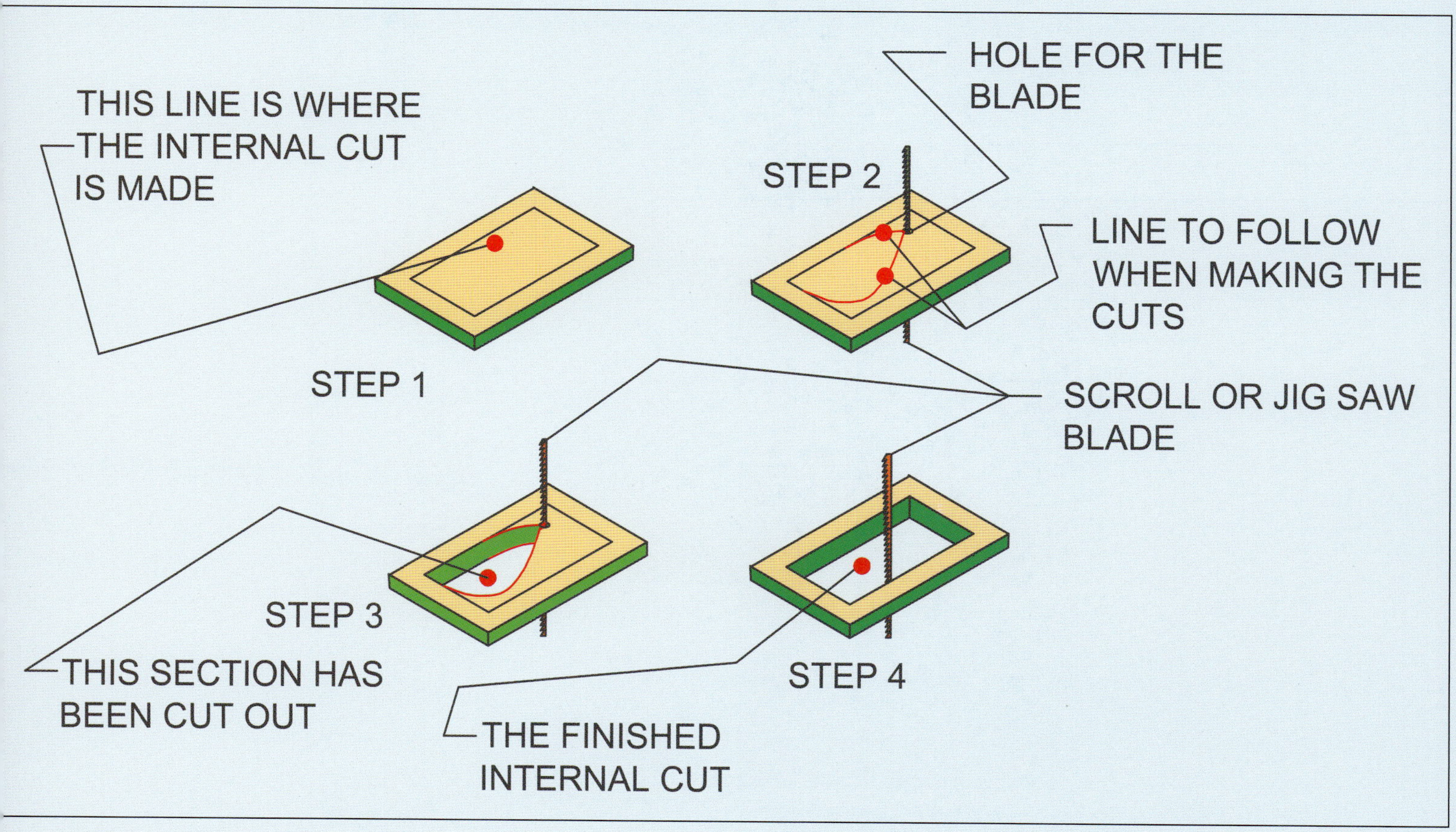

Fig. 2-36

XI. Resawing

Resawing is taking a board and making two or more thinner pieces from the original board. Throughout this book I usually resaw a 3/4" to 7/8" thick board into two pieces. Each of these pieces would be about 5/16" to 3/8" thick after you resaw. Shown in *Fig. 2-37* is a board I have resawed, making two cuts using a table saw. Sometimes the blade will reach all the way through, but on a wider board, like the one shown, it does not. *Figure 2-38* shows getting ready to cut the small remaining section using a band saw. After the band saw cut is made, the board will become two thinner pieces of lumber. *Figure 2-39* shows a different board after it has been cut on the band saw, leaving a slightly raised section in the center. This can be cut flat using a planer or sanded using a belt sander.

Fig. 2-37: Resawing on the table saw.

Fig. 2-38: This board was too wide to be totally resawed on my table saw. Here I am resawing the center part of the board on a band saw.

Fig. 2-39: This board, resawed on both the table saw and the band saw, will require some planing or sanding to make it perfectly flat.

XII. Kreg Pocket Screw System

The Kreg pocket screw system uses a jig to drill a hole at an angle *(Fig. 2-40)*. Once this angular hole has been drilled, the Kreg company offers a variety of screws for hardwoods and softwoods. Shown in *Fig. 2-41* is a Kreg screw with a 6" bit to attach a part to a backer board. Kreg screws use a square bit that fits into a square hole. The screw does not fall off the bit easily. The Kreg company offers a large variety of jigs. These are commonly used for making frames, doors, furniture parts, etc.

Fig. 2-40: Drilling angular holes using a pocket screw jig.

Fig. 2-41: Attaching the bottom part of the frame for an intarsia eagle project using a 6" bit and a pocket screw.

XIII. Compass

If you don't have a compass that will make a large circle, it is easy to make one *(Fig. 2-42)*. Take a long board, drill a hole in the end, in which a standard pencil will fit into tightly. On the other end, drill a series of holes (depending on the size of circle you need) for a nail to fit into tightly. Using this method you can draw a fairly precise arc or circle.

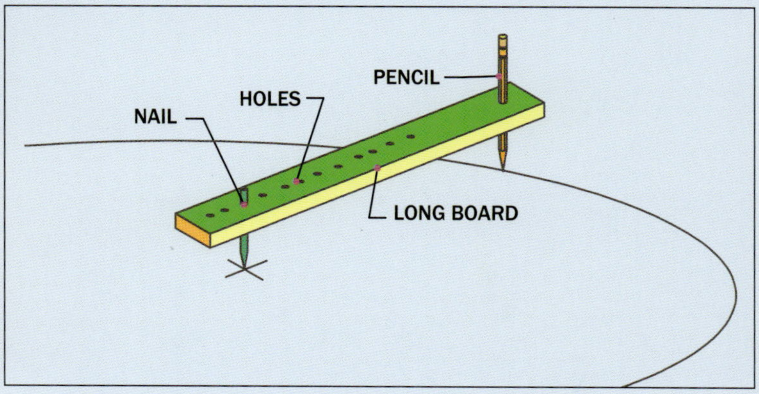

Fig. 2-42

Chapter III

Easy Eagle

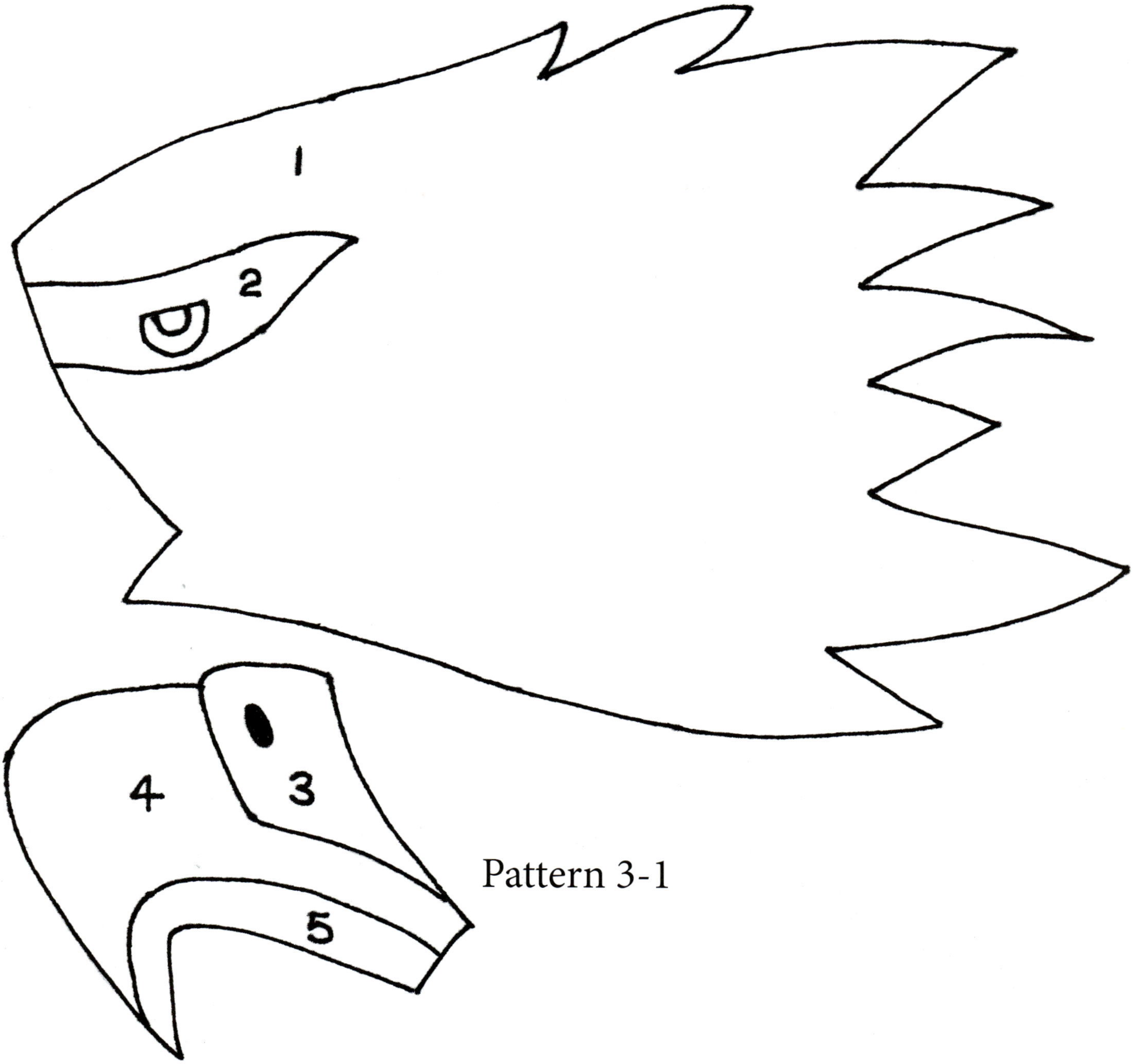

Pattern 3-1

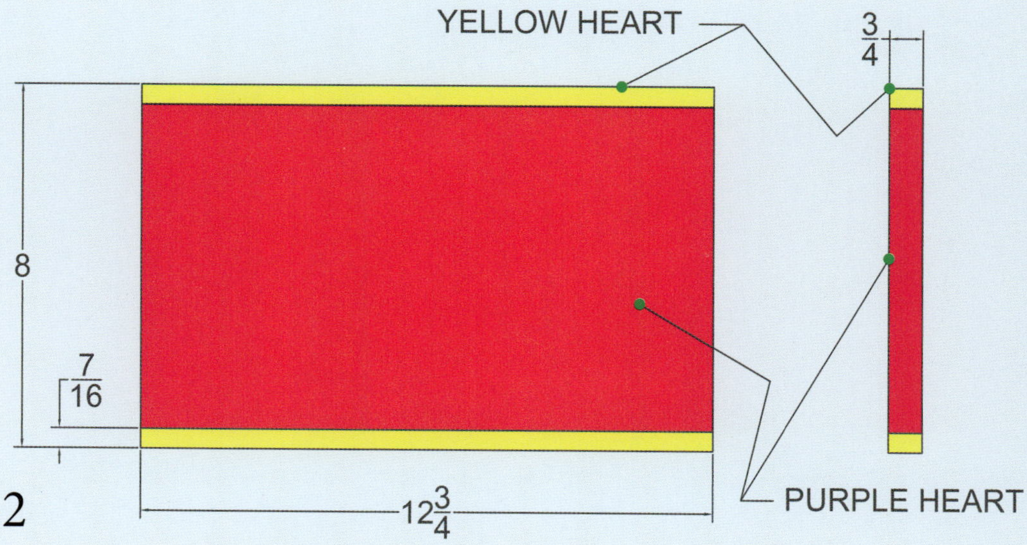

Pattern 3-2

Materials: The Easy Eagle is made from yellow heart, maple, purple heart, and coco bolo.

Refer to *Patterns 3-1 & 3-2* for this eagle.

• The beak is started by resawing or buying a piece of yellow heart that is 1/4 to 3/8" thick; see "Resawing" in Chapter II. Once the yellow heart is sanded *(Fig. 3-1)*, layout parts 3, 4, and 5 *(Fig. 3-2)*.

Fig. 3-1: Sanding with an orbital sander.

Fig. 3-2: Tracing the beak, parts 3, 4, and 5.

• Using a jig saw, cut the outside of part 4 *(Fig. 3-3)*. To obtain a nice sharp corner, cut from two directions *(Fig. 3-4)*. Be sure you are using a thin blade, which will keep the kerf narrow, ensuring the parts will fit together better *(Fig. 3-5)*.

Fig. 3-3: Cutting the beak out on the jig saw.

Fig. 3-4: Using two cuts to make a sharp corner.

Fig. 3-5: Cutting between parts 4 and 5 of the beak.

• Continue by completing the cut for part 5 *(Fig. 3-6)* and then part 4 *(Fig. 3-7)*. Hold the large piece of yellow heart and cut out part 3 *(Fig. 3-8)*.

Fig. 3-6: Part 5, the bottom part of the beak, has been cut out.

Fig. 3-7: Part 4 is completely cut out.

Fig. 3-8: Finally, the entire beak section is cut out.

• Sand these three parts on a Sand-O-Flex sander or by hand *(Fig. 3-9)*. The very small pieces should be held with a pair of pliers while using the Sand-O-Flex *(Fig. 3-10)*.

Fig. 3-9: Holding the piece by hand using the Sand-O-Flex.

Fig. 3-10: Holding a small piece with a pair of pliers while it is being sanded with a Sand-O-Flex.

• When cutting out part 1, set parts 3, 4, and 5 on the maple board and trace the edge of 3, 4, and 5 onto part 1. Then trace the paper pattern to part 1 and cut the section that adjoins parts 3, 4, and 5 *(Fig. 3-11)*. Be sure this fits correctly *(Fig. 3-12)*.
• Cut out the feathers on part 1 by making two cuts for each feather *(Fig. 3-13)* instead of trying to turn a sharp corner. Finish cutting part 1 *(Fig. 3-14)*.
• Now check the fit with the beak section again and sand part 1 *(Figs. 3-15 & Fig. 3-16)*.

Fig. 3-11: The beak section is ready to be fit into the feathers, part 1.

Fig. 3-12: Checking the fit of the beak and the feathers.

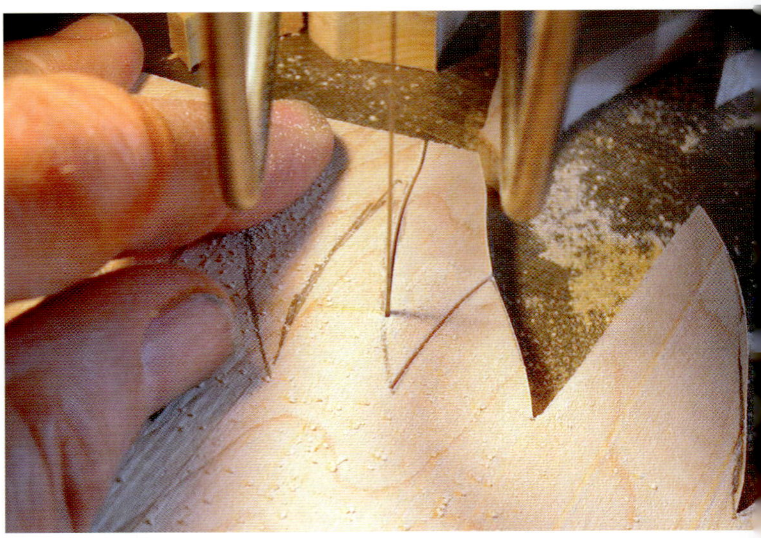

Fig. 3-13: Making two cuts produces a sharper corner.

Fig. 3-14: The outside of the feathers have been cut out.

Fig. 3-15: Again, check the fit between the beak section and the feathers.

Fig. 3-16: Sand any imperfections out on the feathers.

• Trace the paper pattern for part 2 on a dark wood; in this case I used a dark coco bolo although wenge or black ebony would also work well *(Fig. 3-17)*. Cut part 2 out and trace it on the maple for part 1; see "Tracing patterns" in Chapter II *(Figs. 3-18 & 3-19)*. Be sure to cut inside the line while touching the line *(Figs. 3-20 & 3-21)*.

Fig. 3-17: Use a paper pattern to trace the eye section, part 2.

Fig. 3-18: Using a very sharp pencil, trace the eye section onto the feathers.

Fig. 3-19: The eye section has been traced.

Fig. 3-20: Do not cut the line off; cut closely inside the line.

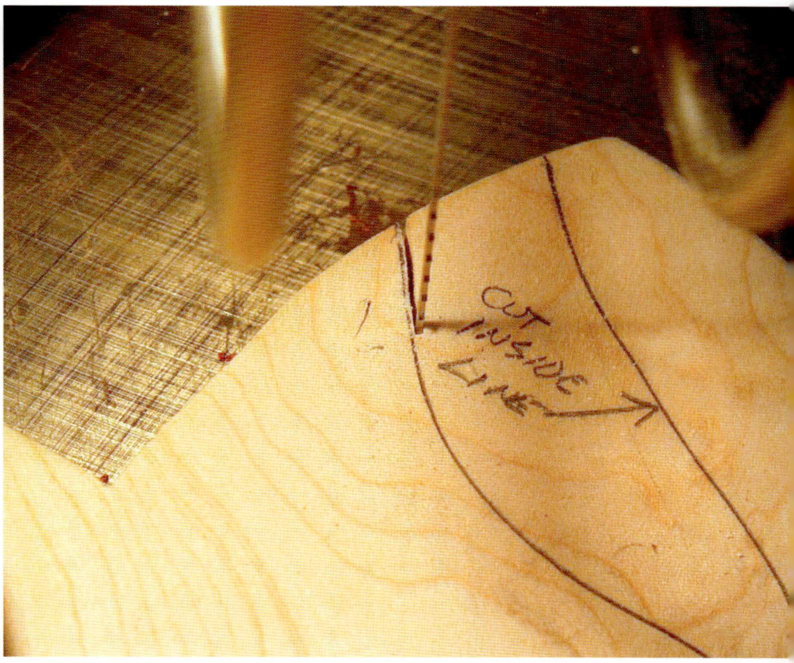

Fig. 3-21: Using a scroll saw, cut inside the line.

• Once this is cut out, try fitting part 2 into part 1, *(Figs. 3-22 & 3-23).*

• Using a drill press and a plug cutter, make three or four, 1/2" plugs of yellow heart *(Fig. 3-24).* Only one is needed, but make a few extra in case one breaks. Then, using a 1/4" drill bit, drill a hole in each plug about 3/8" deep *(Fig. 3-25).* Again, using a drill press, cut several 1/4" plugs out of a dark wood; coco bolo is shown *(Fig. 3-26).* These plugs can be easily removed by using a screw driver *(Figs. 3-27 & 3-28).*

Fig. 3-22: Placing the eye section into the cavity you have just cut.

Fig. 3-25: Drilling the hole for the pupil.

Fig. 3-23: This photo shows a nice fit.

Fig. 3-26: Making plugs to be used for the pupil.

Fig. 3-24: Making plugs using a drill press.

Fig. 3-27: Using a screw driver to wedge the plugs out.

• Glue these into the yellow heart plugs making several eyes *(Fig. 3-29)*. Notice one plug is broken, so it is a good thing I made several extra. Don't worry about the excess glue, it can be removed later. Once the eyes are dry, sand them on a disc sander *(Figs. 3-30 & Fig. 3-31)*.

Fig. 3-28: The plugs should pop out easily.

Fig. 3-30: Sanding the plugs smooth with a disc sander.

Fig. 3-29: The plug has been glued into the yellow heart. Notice I made a few extra.

Fig. 3-31: The finished plug before it is cut out of the yellow heart.

• Draw a parallel line about 1/16 to 3/32" in from the edge of the material *(Fig. 3-32)*. Using a band saw, slowly cut along the line; the eyes will pop out *(Fig. 3-33)*. I suggest using a small scrap piece of wood to lay on the band saw's table to catch the eyes *(Fig. 3-34)*. Notice I have extra eyes; keep them and maybe you will need them on another project *(Fig. 3-35)*. Holding it with a pair of pliers, sand the side of one eye flat on the disc sander *(Fig. 3-36)*. Using the pliers will give you a better grip and it is much safer than holding a small piece with your fingers. Check your progress so far *(Fig. 3-37)*. Using a thick and clear CA glue, glue the eye on *(Fig. 3-38)*.

Fig. 3-32: This photo shows a pencil line where we will make a cut with the band saw.

Fig. 3-33: The eyes will fall out as you cut the piece on the band saw.

Fig. 3-34: Notice the board that keeps the eyes from falling through the throat of your band saw.

Fig. 3-35: I usually save this piece of wood and use it for eyes on other projects.

Fig. 3-36: Flattening the eye on one side with a pair of pliers and a disc sander.

Fig. 3-37: Place the eye on the eagle and mark where it goes. This photo shows progress thus far.

• The backer board is made of a piece of purple heart with yellow heart on the sides. Glue this up as shown in *Fig. 3-39*. Once this is dry, cut it to length and sand *(Fig. 3-40)*. Mark the exact placement of the eagle *(Fig. 3-41)*. Notice that I have marked two marks. An outside line, which is the tracing of the actual eagle and an inside line, which is where the glue should stop *(Fig. 3-42)*.

Fig. 3-38: Using a thick CA glue, glue the eagle eye on.

Fig. 3-39: Gluing yellow heart strips to the purple heart using bar clamps.

Fig. 3-40: The completed backer board.

Fig. 3-41: Mark the spot where you will glue the eagle on.

Fig. 3-42: Make a second mark, about 1/4 to 3/8" inside the traced line.

• Spread the glue out, I use titebond glue. DO NOT USE TOO MUCH GLUE, PREVENT SQUEEZE OUT *(Fig. 3-43)*. Glue all the parts onto the purple heart *(Fig. 3-44)*. Remove the squeeze out glue with a knife *(Fig. 3-45)*. Burn the nose hole for the eagle, on part 3, with a woodburner or use a black permanent marker after you have put the finish on. At this point the construction of your project should be done and you are ready to apply a finish. I like to use a spray can of lacquer. For hanging your eagle see "Hangers" in Chapter II.

Fig. 3-43: Apply glue inside the second mark.

Fig. 3-44: Glue the beak next.

Fig. 3-45: Use a knife to remove any excess glue.

Chapter IV

Twenty-Four Inch Eagle

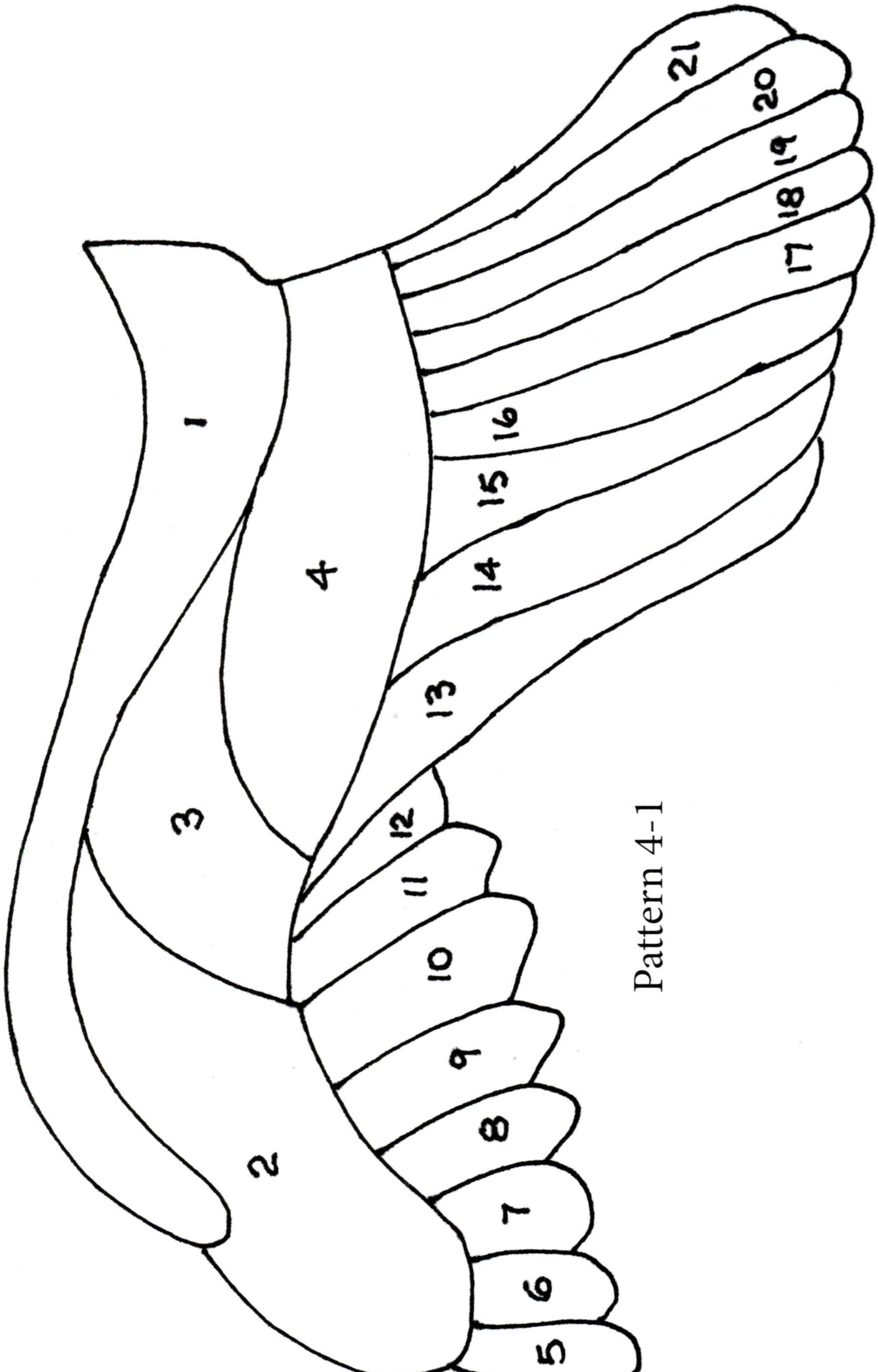

Pattern 4-1

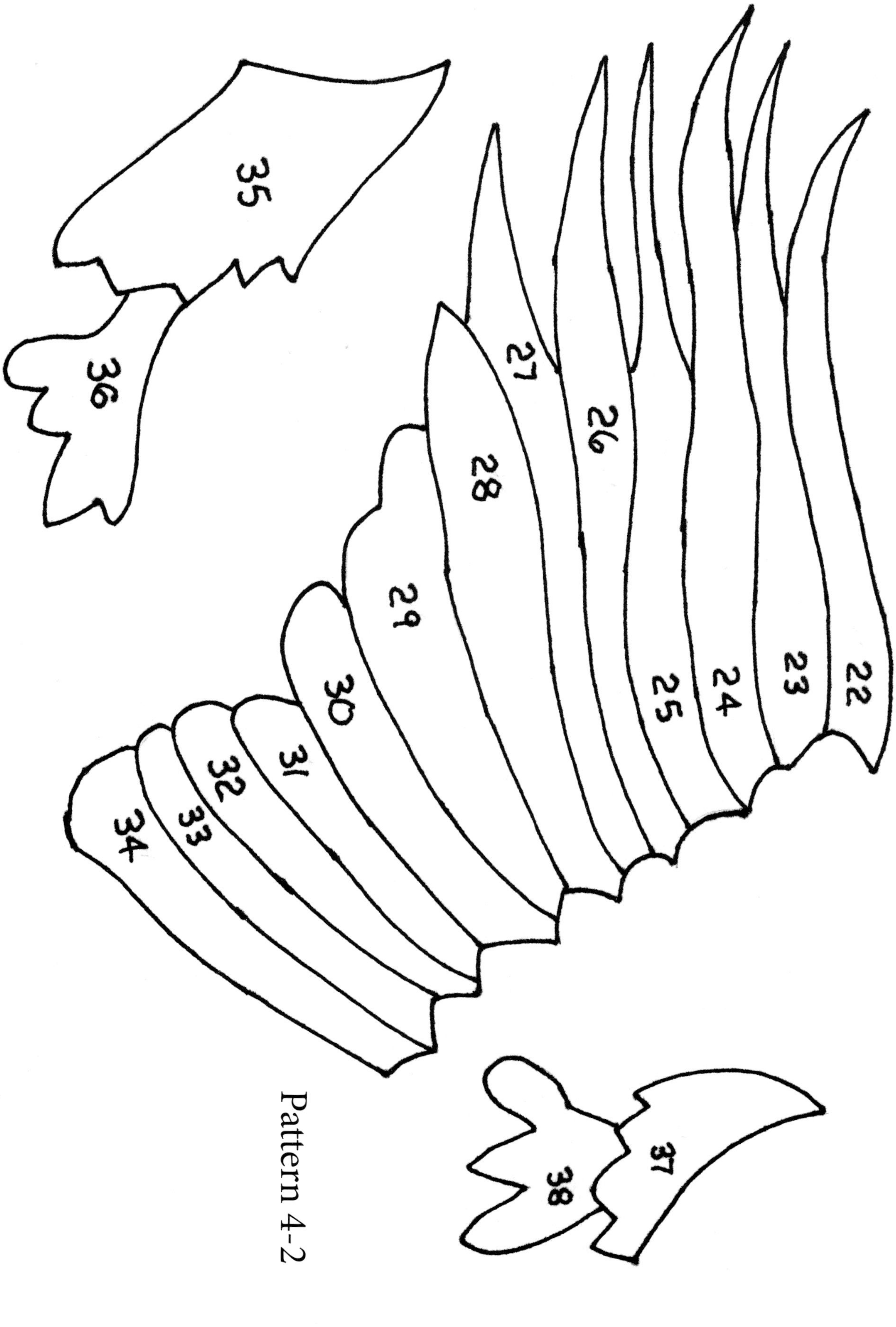

Pattern 4-2

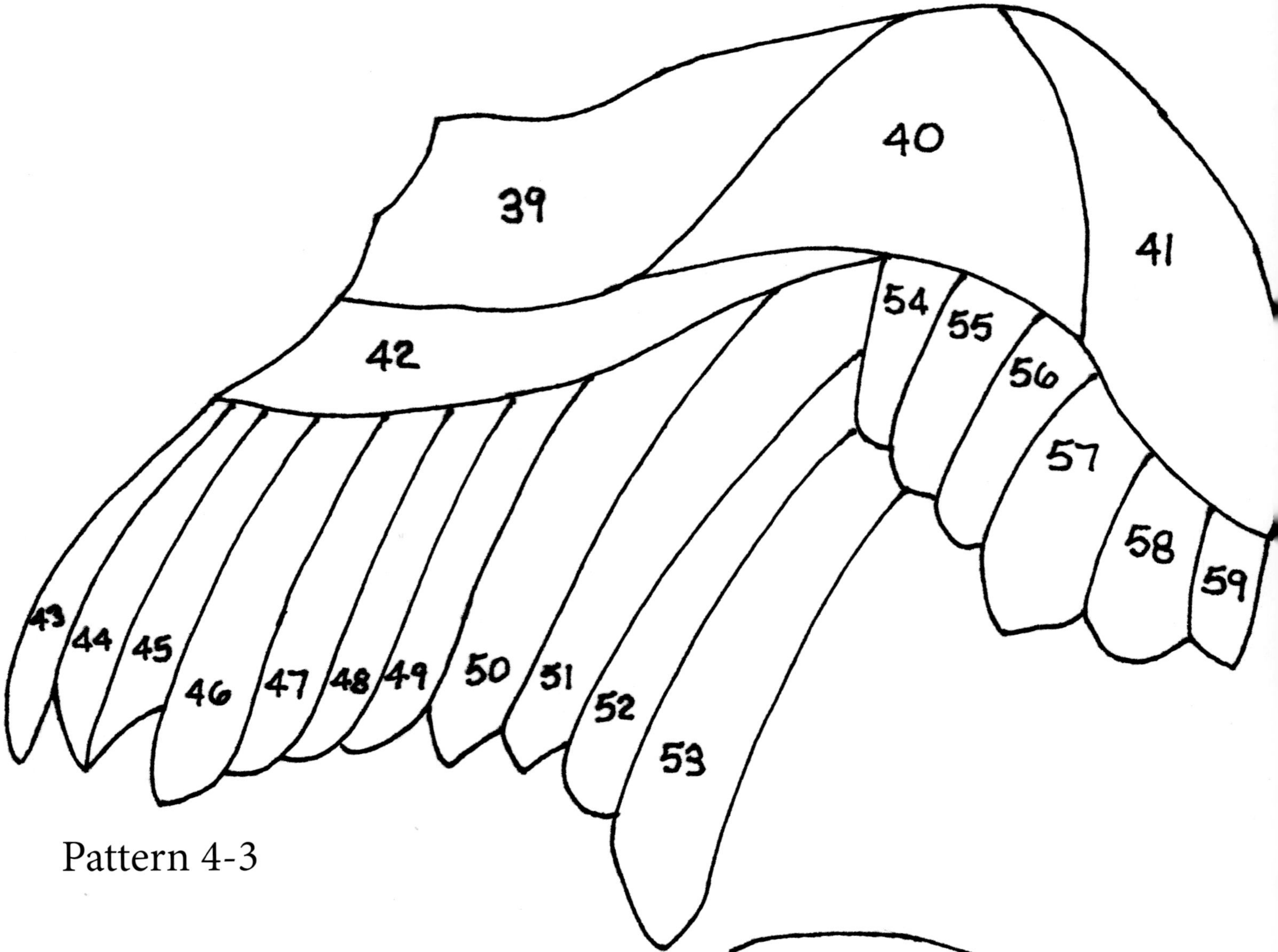

Pattern 4-3

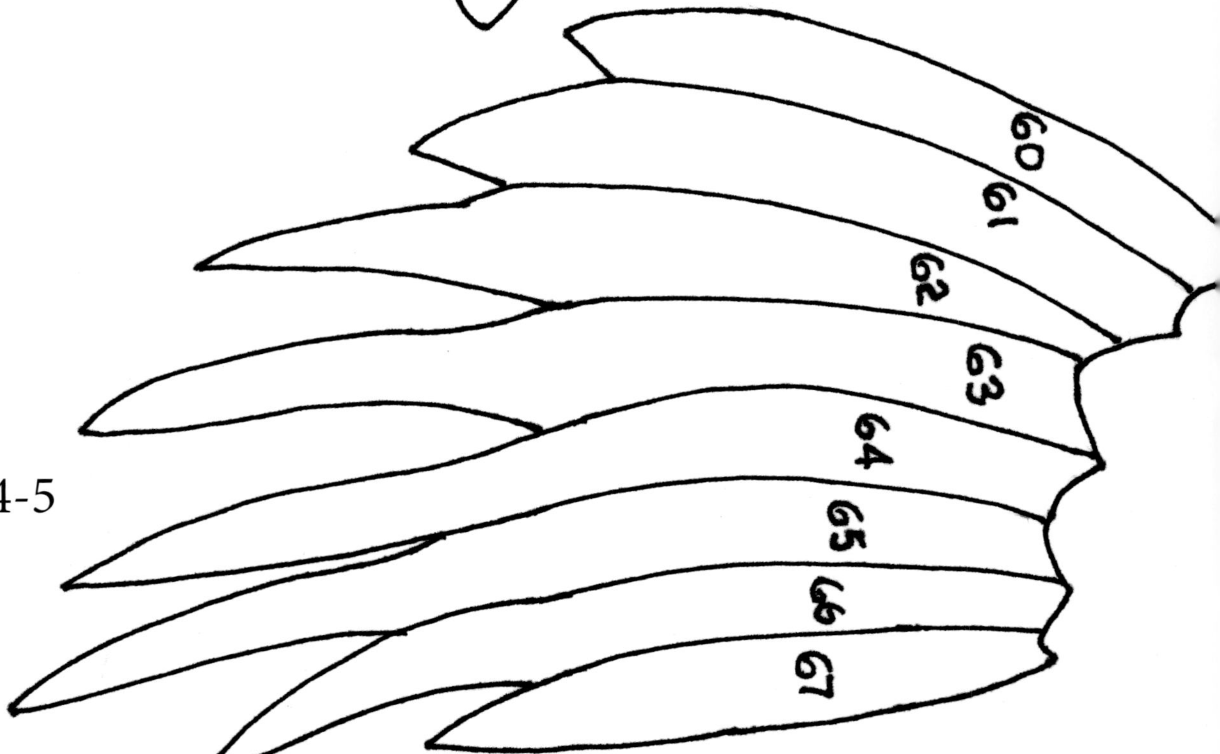

Pattern 4-5

Pattern 4-4

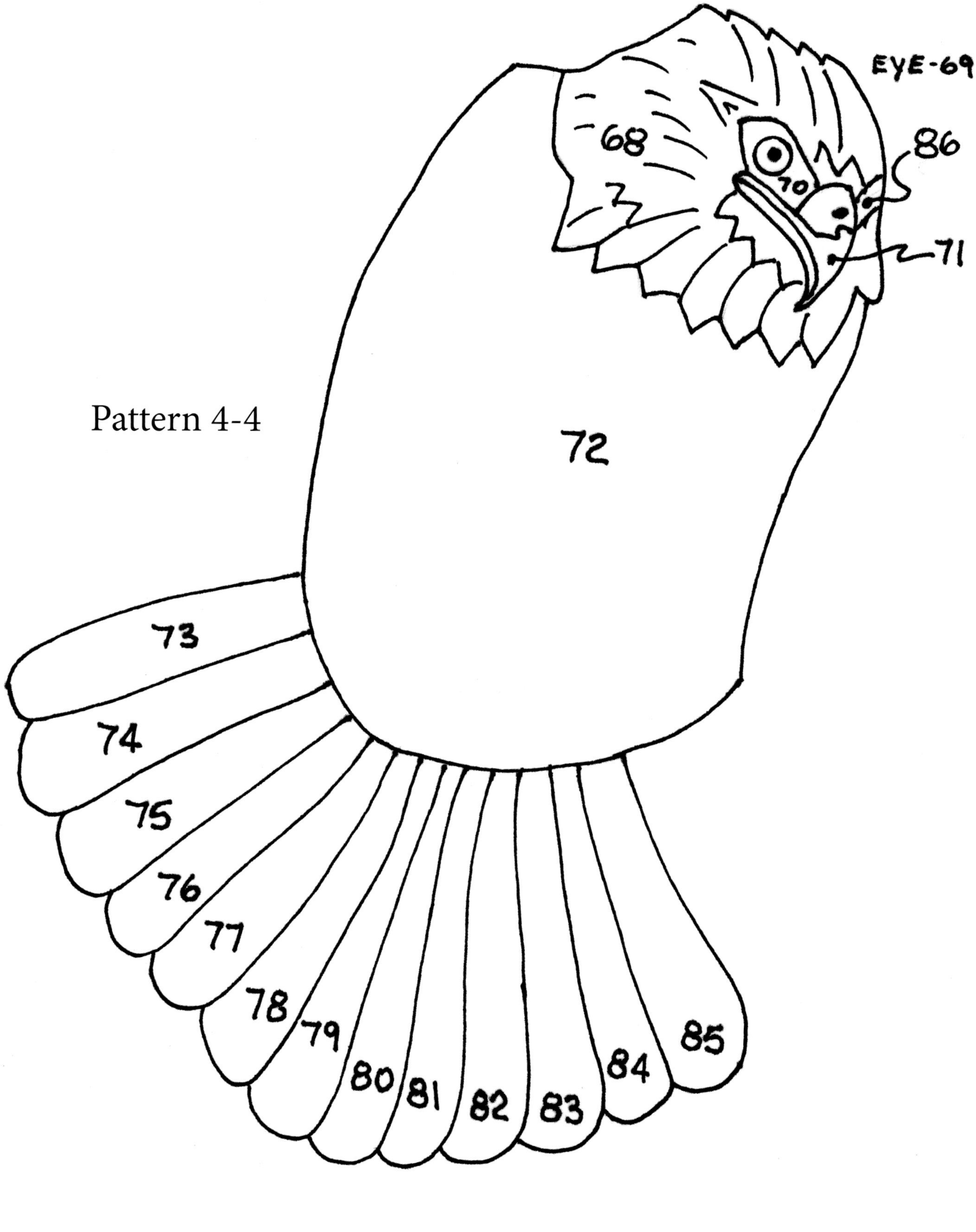

Materials: The Twenty-Four Inch Eagle gets its name because it's approximately 24 inches wide wing tip to wing tip. The woods used for this eagle are jatoba, cottonwood, spalted maple, cherry, yellow heart, and black ebony.

Refer to *Patterns 4-1* to *4-5* for this eagle.

• Start this project by making the left wing. I have resawed my material to make it 9/16 to 5/8" thick. See "Resawing" in Chapter II. Parts 1, 2, 3, 4, 39, 40, 41, and 42 are made of jatoba. When I made this part for the left wing I also made the corresponding right wing parts. Trace these parts on a piece of jatoba. In the picture you may notice that I'm using a piece of tongue and groove flooring; notice the tongue on one side of the wood *(Fig. 4-1)*. Cut out parts 1, 2, 3, 4, as one piece of wood *(Fig. 4-2)*. In the photograph, I am using a band saw. Then cut out the individual pieces for parts 1, 2, 3, and 4 *(Fig. 4-3)*. When I get to a sharp curve that is tight on the band saw, I finish the cut using a thinner jig saw or scroll saw blade, *(Figs. 4-4, 4-5, & 4-6)*. Sand a slightly rounded edge on each of these parts *(Fig. 4-7)*. You can use a drum sander or the end of a belt sander.

Fig. 4-1: Tracing the pattern for parts 1 through 4.

Fig. 4-2: Cutting around the outside of parts 1 through 4 on the band saw.

Fig. 4-3: Cutting out part 4.

Fig. 4-4: Cutting out part 1.

Fig. 4-5: Cutting the sharp corner on part 1 must be done on a jig saw.

Fig. 4-6: Part 1 is completely cut out.

• When cutting parts 39, 40, and 42 for the right wing, notice that the grain in part 41 goes in a different direction *(Fig. 4-8)*. Both left and right wings, part 1 to 4 and 39 to 42 are shown in *Fig. 4-9*. The left wing has been sanded which enhances the line. Sand both wings to this finished state *(Fig. 4-10)*.

• Since the body, part 72, is made out of jatoba, I had to glue two pieces of wood together *(Fig. 4-11)*. I like to glue small pieces like this in an old vice, but a variety of clamps would work just as well *(Fig. 4-12)*. While these two parts are drying, continue to work on the left wing.

Fig. 4-7: Sand these parts using the end of a belt sander or a drum sander.

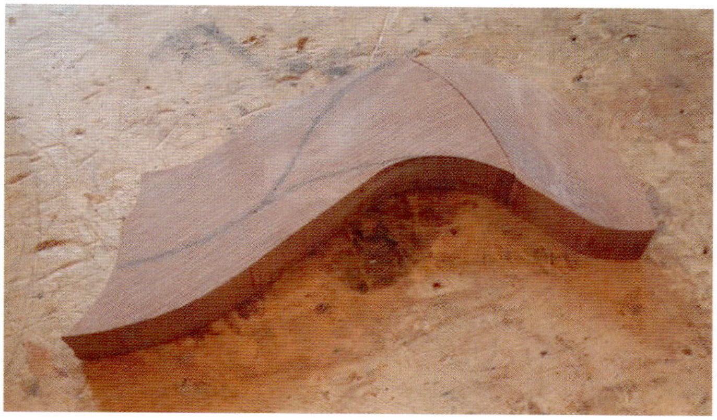

Fig. 4-8: Parts 39 through 41. Notice the different grain direction for 41.

Fig. 4-9: Here, parts 1 through 4 have been sanded. Parts 39 through 41 have not.

Fig. 4-10: Parts 1 through 4 and parts 39 through 41 have been sanded and show a nice rounded joint between each part.

Fig. 4-11: Gluing two parts wide enough to make the body, part 72.

Fig. 4-12: These are clamped in an old vice until they dry.

• Next, make parts 13 to 21 out of cherry. Instead of tracing the paper pattern for the top section of these parts, I used the already made parts 2, 3, and 4 to trace the top section *(Fig. 4-13)*. Cut out these parts as shown in *Fig. 4-14*, making sure you have a good fit with parts 1, 2, and 3 as shown *(Fig. 4-15)*. Trace parts 13 through 21 on the face of this board. Notice I have numbered the parts *(Fig. 4-16)* to make it easy to assemble. These numbers, 1 through 9, do not correspond with the drawing numbers but are only drawn on the piece of wood to make them easy to assemble. If you happen to drop these and they are not numbered they can be like a miniature jigsaw puzzle to reassemble. Cut these out. I like to use a jig saw since it makes a thinner kerf *(Fig. 4-17)*. Follow the same procedure for parts 5 through 12 *(Fig. 4-18)*. Use part 13 for tracing part 12 in the same manner as previously described *(Fig. 4-19)*. Be sure these parts fit correctly *(Fig. 4-20)*. Cut out parts 5 through 12 using a scroll saw *(Fig. 4-21)*. Make all your cuts in one direction, then cut in the other direction, *(Fig. 4-22)*. I think this is quicker than doing one at a time. Finish cutting parts 5 through 12 *(Figs. 4-23 & 4-24)*. These small pieces can be sanded on a Sand-O-Flex using a pair of pliers to hold them *(Fig. 4-25)*.

Fig. 4-13: Using parts 4 and 1 to trace where parts 13 through 21 intersect.

Fig. 4-16: Marking the bottom of these feathers so they can be easily put together.

Fig. 4-14: Cutting out parts 13 through 21 as one unit.

Fig. 4-17: Cutting out parts 13 through 21 using a thin blade on a jig saw.

Fig. 4-15: Making sure parts 13 through 21 fit nicely against parts 3 and 4.

Fig. 4-18: Tracing the edge of parts 2 and 3 to intersect with parts 5 through 12.

Fig. 4-19: Tracing part 13 where it will intersect with part 12.

Fig. 4-23: Cutting out the individual parts 5 through 12.

Fig. 4-20: Cutting out parts 5 through 12 as a unit, making sure it fits correctly.

Fig. 4-24: The parts cut thus far are shown fitting together nicely.

Fig. 4-21: Cutting out the feather tips in one direction.

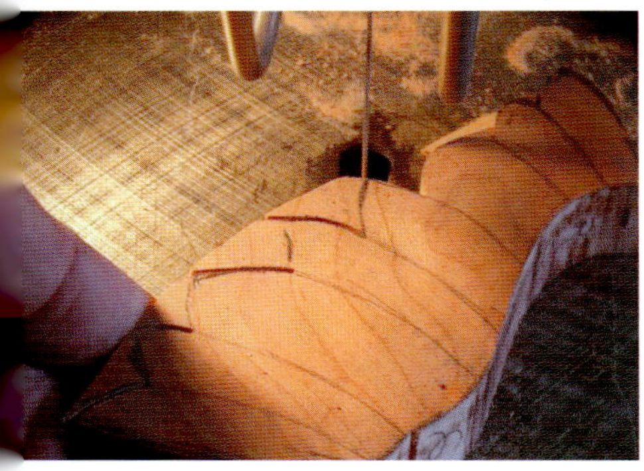

Fig. 4-22: Making the second cut on the tip of the feathers, parts 5 through 12.

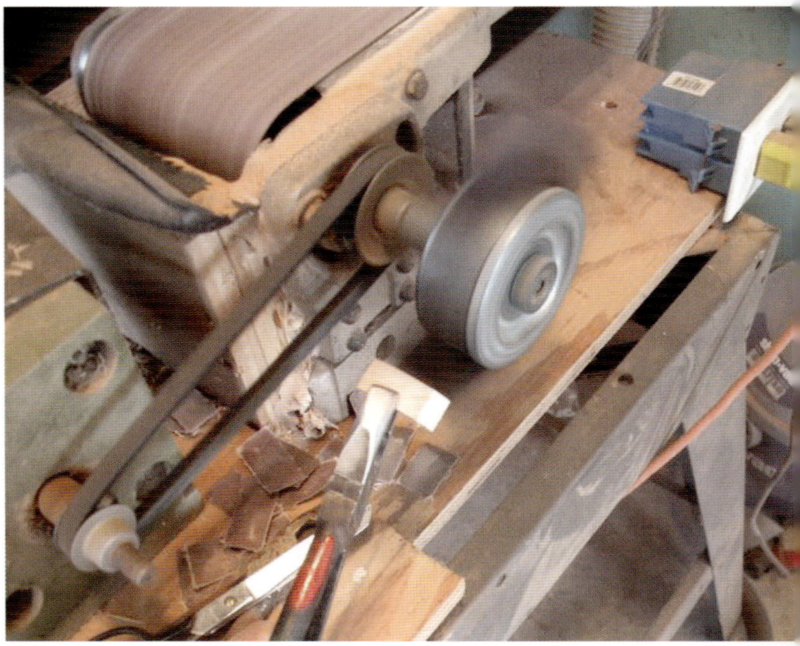

Fig. 4-25: I sand small parts, holding them with a pair of pliers, on a Sand-O-Flex.

• *Figure 4-26* shows the progress on the right wing to this point. It is difficult to keep all of these little parts together without dislodging them, so to solve this, I use a paper backing made with a manila folder. Spread some titebond glue out using a scrap block *(Figs. 4-27 & 4-28)*. Then glue the parts 1 to 21 to this paper *(Figs. 4-29 & 4-30)*. Once this is done and dried, cut away the excess paper *(Fig. 4-31)*, now these parts should stay together as one unit. *Figure 4-32*, shows the back of the left wing as a unit thus far.

Fig. 4-26: Parts 1 through 21 have been sanded and fitted together.

Fig. 4-27: Spreading glue on a piece of manila paper to temporarily glue parts 1 through 21.

Fig. 4-28: Spreading the glue out with a scrap piece of wood.

Fig. 4-29: Gluing parts 1 through 4 to the paper.

Fig. 4-30: Gluing parts 5 through 21 to the manila paper.

Fig. 4-31: Cutting the paper away after the glue is thoroughly dry.

• Continue by making parts 22 through 34 *(Fig. 4-33)*. Again, I use the method of tracing the edge of intersecting parts instead of tracing from the pattern. When this fits nicely *(Fig. 4-34)*, continue cutting the feathers out until the left wing is finished *(Fig. 4-35)*. Use the same process to build the right wing.

Fig. 4-32: This shows the backside of part 1 through 21 glued to the manila paper.

Fig. 4-33: Parts 5 and 6 broke off and will need to be reglued with a small scrap of paper.

Fig. 4-34: Making parts 22 through 34, fitting them against the previously made parts.

Fig. 4-35: The completed left wing.

• With both left and right wings finished, start the body, part 72. Trace the edge on each side of the body, as shown in *Fig. 4-36*, and finish tracing with the paper pattern *(Fig. 4-37)*. Cut the sides first and be sure they fit snugly with the wing *(Fig. 4-38)*. You may have to undercut a little bit as shown *(Fig. 4-39)*. See "Undercutting Parts" in Chapter II. Check the fit for the right wing *(Fig. 4-40)*. *Figure 4-41* shows the progress thus far.

Fig. 4-36: Using the left wing and the right wing to trace part 72, the body.

Fig. 4-37: The body after it has been traced.

Fig. 4-38: Part 72 has been cut out making sure it fits against the right wing.

Fig. 4-39: Shows a slight undercut, used to insure a good fit.

Fig. 4-40: Holding the right wing against the body and adjusting the fit.

Fig. 4-41: Both wings have been fit to part 72.

• Place a piece of cottonwood underneath the body, part 72. Using a paper pattern, trace the head onto the cottonwood *(Fig. 4-42)*. Cut this out and get a good fit *(Figs. 4-43 & 4-44)*. If you are a little off like I was, draw a line to be cut *(Figs. 4-45 & 4-46)*. Notice the line is very close to the original cut.

In *Fig. 4-47*, notice that I am barely cutting the edge. Now, the two parts fit better. At this point, finish cutting out the rest of the head, *(Figs. 4-48 & 4-49)*. *Figure 4-50* shows the two parts fitted together. *Figure 4-51* shows the head with its adjoining parts fitting correctly.

Fig. 4-42: Tracing the head of the eagle using a paper pattern, part 72, and both wings.

Fig. 4-47: A very fine cut is required. Notice that I am barely cutting the edge.

Figs. 4-43 & 4-44: Part of the head has been cut out to fit the body.

Figs. 4-48 & 4-49: Cutting the top part of the eagle's head.

Figs. 4-45 & 4-46: Making an adjustment mark to recut to insure a better fit.

Fig. 4-50: Shows the head fitting into the body.

Fig. 4-51: The body, head, and wings fitting together.

• Resaw a piece of yellow heart to about 1/16" thick for the beak *(Fig. 4-52)*. Notice that I have used a much longer board than I need for resawing, but it keeps my hands away from the blade—a much safer operation. You will need a piece of yellow heart about 2 or 3" long, which is much longer than what you need when cutting on a jig saw. Trace the pattern for the beak *(Figs. 4-53 & 4-54)*. When I cut small parts like this, I use a thin blade *(Fig. 4-55)*. Cut the beak out *(Fig. 4-56)*. I like to use a piece of 3/4" plywood on the table of the scroll saw, which prevents small pieces from falling through the throat *(Figs. 4-57 & 4-58)*.

Fig. 4-52: Resawing a piece of yellow heart.

Fig. 4-55: Use a thin blade (like the one on the left) to cut this out.

Fig. 4-56: Cutting out the beak on the jig saw.

Fig. 4-53: Preparing to trace the beak on the yellow heart.

Fig. 4-57: Using a piece of plywood underneath the beak so the beak will not fall through the throat of the jig saw.

Fig. 4-54: The beak has been traced on the yellow heart.

Fig. 4-58: Continue cutting out the beak.

• Next cut out part 70 which is made out of spalted maple *(Fig. 4-59)*. You may notice part 70 is a little thicker than the beak, this can be sanded down later. Mark the location of the beak, part 71, and glue it down *(Figs. 4-60 & 4-61)*. It is not necessary to clamp this. Glue part 70 down. In *Fig. 4-62* I am using a knife to get off any squeezed out glue. *Figure 4-63* shows the progress to this point.

Fig. 4-59: Shows the beak and the eye section, part 70, as they fit together.

Fig. 4-60: Place these on the head and mark their positions on the cottonwood.

Fig. 4-61: Gluing the beak and eye section to the head. Press these down using titebond glue. Clamping should not be necessary.

• Make part 86 *(Fig. 4-64)* and glue it on. Sand the end that sticks over the head so it is flush on its side and then sand all three parts till they are flush on top *(Fig. 4-65)*.

Fig. 4-62: Removing excess glue with a knife.

Fig. 4-63: The eagle's progress thus far.

Fig. 4-64: Drawing part 86.

Fig. 4-65: Sanding part 86, 70, and 71 flush.

• To make the eye of the eagle, use a drill press and plug cutter. Make several plugs that are 5/16" in diameter *(Fig. 4-66)*. Drill a 1/8" diameter hole in the center of each of these plugs *(Fig. 4-67)*. The edge of one plug broke off while drilling, that is why I make several eyes. Fill the 1/8" holes with InLace *(Figs. 4-68 & 4-69)*. Let this dry overnight.

Fig. 4-66: Using a drill press with a plug cutter to cut the plug for the eye.

Fig. 4-68: InLace can be used for the pupil.

Fig. 4-67: Using a twist bit to drill the hole for the pupil.

Fig. 4-69: Applying InLace in several plugs.

• While the InLace is drying you can make parts 35, 36, 37 and 38. These parts should only be about 5/16" thick. Use the body, part 72, and the pattern to trace part 35 *(Fig. 4-70)*. Cut out parts 35 and 37 *(Fig. 4-71)*. Make sure parts 35 and 37 fit correctly. Notice that my cottonwood is not wide enough to make all the feathers *(Fig. 4-72)*. *Figure 4-73* shows gluing two pieces of cottonwood together. While the cottonwood is drying, cut out parts 36 and 38 *(Fig. 4-74)*. Notice that parts 36 and 38 are slightly thinner than 35 and 37 *(Fig. 4-75)*. *Figure 4-76* shows the progress of the eagle thus far.

Fig. 4-70: Tracing part 35 using part 72 to insure a good fit.

Fig. 4-71: Part 35 has been cut out.

Fig. 4-72: Parts 35 and 72 fit nicely.

Fig. 4-73: Gluing two, 1/4" thick pieces of cottonwood together for the tail feathers.

Fig. 4-74: Cutting part 36 and fitting it to part 35.

Fig. 4-75: Parts 36 and 35 fitting correctly.

Fig. 4-76: Shows the parts of the eagle completed thus far.

• Use a file to sharpen your woodburner *(Fig. 4-77)*. Burn the lines in parts 35 and 37 *(Fig. 4-78)*. Burn the feather lines in the head *(Fig. 4-79)*. *Figure 4-80* shows the progress on the eagle to this point.

• By this time the eyes may be dry. So sand them smooth on one side using a disc sander *(Fig. 4-81)*. You may need to remove some excess InLace around the outside of the eye. Do this with a plug cutter on the drill press *(Figs. 4-82 & 4-83)*. Mark a line about 3/32" from the edge of this piece of yellow heart as shown in *Fig. 4-84*. Cut along this line and the eyes should fall out *(Figs. 4-85 & 4-86)*. Put a small drop of thick, clear CA glue where the eye goes on the eagle *(Fig. 4-87)*. Glue the eye on. Remove any excess glue *(Fig. 4-88)*.

Fig. 4-77: Using a file to sharpen the woodburner.

Fig. 4-80: The eagle after using the woodburner.

Fig. 4-78: Burning the lines in part 35.

Fig. 4-79: Burning the feather lines in the face.

Fig. 4-81: Sanding the InLace in the eye.

Fig. 4-82: Removing excess InLace using the original plug cutter.

Fig. 4-83: Making three eyes—only one is needed for this project.

Fig. 4-84: The pencil line is used as a cutting guide for removing the eyes.

Fig. 4-85: Starting to cut out eyes on the band saw.

Fig. 4-86: Use a scrap board to catch the eyes as they pop out.

Fig. 4-87: Use a small drop of clear thick CA glue to glue the eye on.

Fig. 4-88: Removing excess glue.

• After the cottonwood is dry, sand it with an orbital sander *(Fig. 4-89)*. Layout the feathers with your paper pattern, parts 73 through 85, and cut them. Number them on the back *(Fig. 4-90)*. These numbers do not correspond with the drawing numbers; their sole purpose is to make the feathers easy to put together in case you drop them. Cut these out on a scroll saw *(Fig. 4-91)*. Be sure they fit correctly *(Fig. 4-92)*. Then lay parts 35, 36, 37, and 38 on top of them *(Fig. 4-93)*.

Fig. 4-89: Sanding the glued cottonwood smooth.

Fig. 4-90: Numbering the tail feathers for reassembling.

Fig. 4-91: Tail feathers are cutout on the jig saw.

Fig. 4-92: Make sure the tail feathers fit the eagle correctly.

Fig. 4-93: Place parts 35, 36, 37, and 38 on the feathers, making sure they fit correctly.

• To make the backer board see "Backer Board" in Chapter II for detailed instructions. I use a piece of 1/4" oak or birch plywood, lauan works well also. Trace the edge of the eagle onto the 1/4" material. Notice I have a cut line where the long feathers go on the right wing *(Fig. 4-94)*. I will cut the backer board off here. Mark a dark line about 1/4 to 1/2" inside the line you just traced around the eagle, *(Fig. 4-95)*. Do this for the whole eagle. Cut the backer board out *(Fig. 4-96)*. Glue all parts of the eagle to the backer board *(Figs. 4-97 & 4-98)*.

Fig. 4-94: Tracing around the eagle for the backer board. I have cut the plywood short on the right side.

Fig. 4-95: The tracing line and the cut line for the right wing.

Fig. 4-96: The completed 1/4" backer board.

Fig. 4-97: Placing the parts on the backer board, checking the fit.

Fig. 4-98: Gluing parts on using titebond glue. Scrap boards are used to hold the wing up on the right side as well as a couple of tail feathers.

• I use black ebony for the claws. Resaw a piece of black ebony about 3" long that can be used for the claws *(Fig. 4-99)*. To cut the claws out I use a piece of 3/4" plywood, as I have done previously, so the claws do not fall through the throat plate *(Fig. 4-100)*. Use a thick, clear CA glue to glue on the claws *(Figs. 4-101, 4-102, & Fig. 4-103)*. The finished eagle is in *Fig. 4-104*.

Fig. 4-99: A 1/16" piece of black ebony resawed to make the talons.

Fig. 4-100: Cutting out talons on the jig saw. I've used a piece of plywood underneath to prevent the small talons from falling through the throat plate.

Fig. 4-101: Preparing to glue talons on using a dab of clear, thick CA glue.

Fig. 4-102: The first talon glued to part 38.

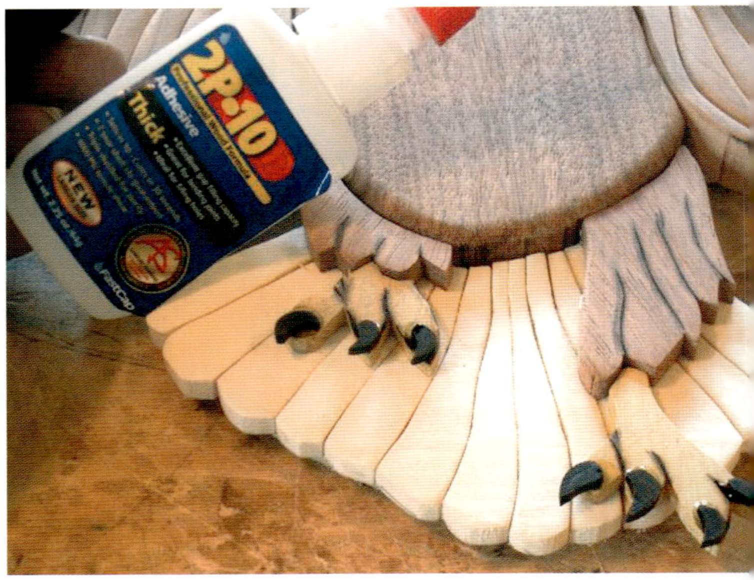

Fig. 4-103: All talons glued into place on parts 38 and 36.

Fig. 4-104: The completed eagle.

Chapter V

The Stern Eagle

Materials: The Stern Eagle is made from blood wood, which is the red colored wood. The white wood is cottonwood. Yellow heart is the yellow wood and the black wood is wenge.

Refer to *Patterns 5-1 & 5-2* for this eagle.

Pattern 5-1

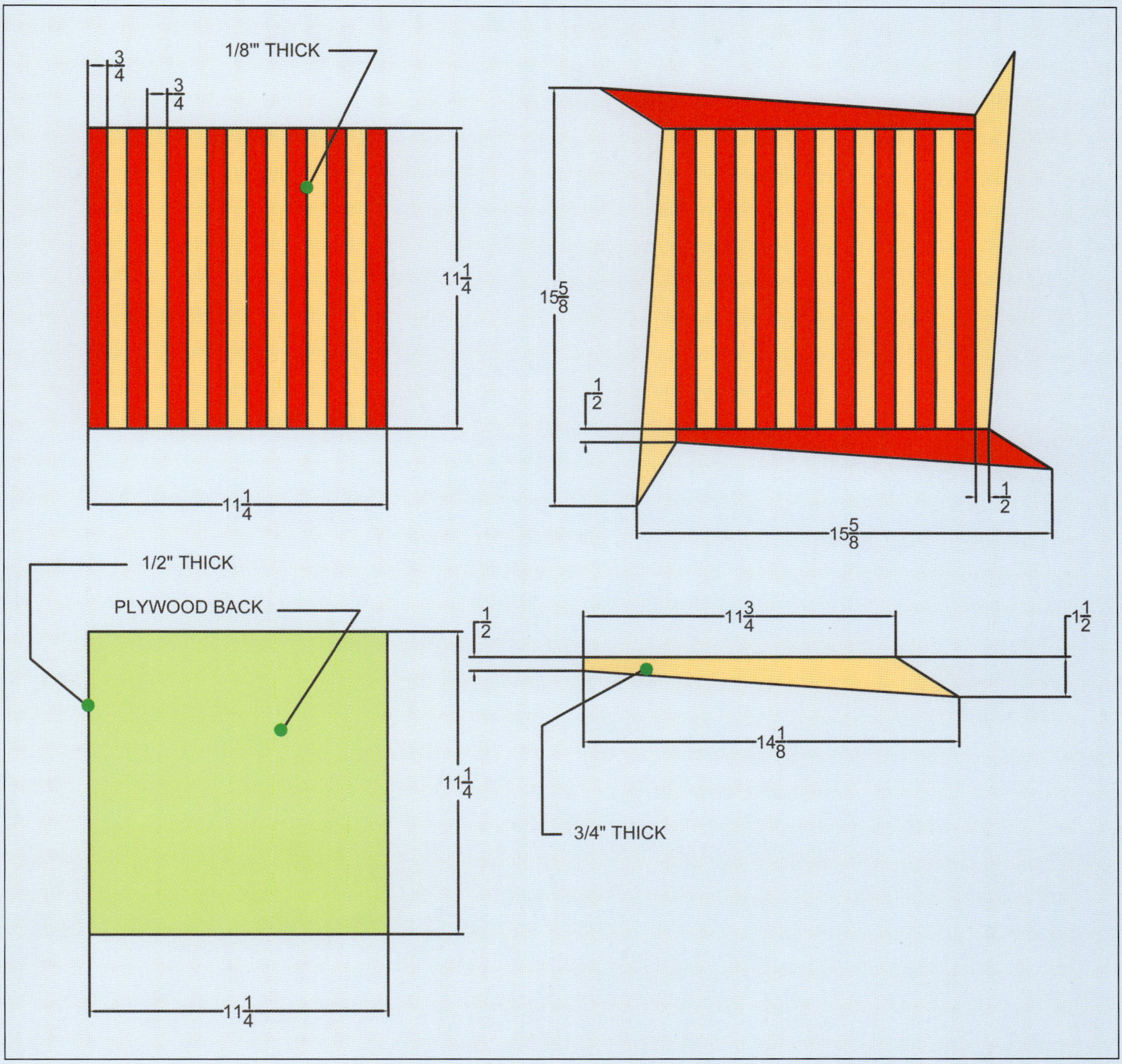
1/8" THICK
3/4
3/4
11 1/4
11 1/4
15 5/8
15 5/8
1/2
1/2
1/2" THICK
PLYWOOD BACK
11 1/4
11 1/4
1/2
11 3/4
1 1/2
14 1/8
3/4" THICK

Pattern 5-2

• The blood wood that I use for the project is 3/4" thick. Use the table saw and cut enough strips for your project. You need eight, 12" long red strips, 1/8" thick *(Fig. 5-1)*. Cut enough cottonwood strips to 1/8" thickness *(Fig. 5-2)*. Use wax paper to protect your table and glue these as shown *(Fig. 5-3)*. Be sure your white and red strips will line up correctly. A red strip will require a white strip next to it *(Fig. 5-4)*. Glue these to a piece of 1/2" plywood *(Fig. 5-5)*. *Figure 5-6* shows clamping these pieces to the plywood. Scrape the hardened excess glue off with a glue scraper *(Fig. 5-7)*.

Fig. 5-1: Bloodwood strips ripped on a table saw.

Fig. 5-2: Bloodwood and cottonwood strips.

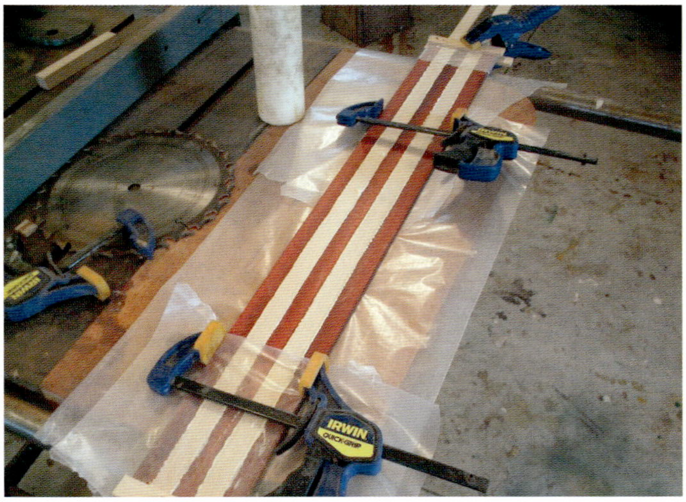

Fig. 5-3: Gluing 5 strips together.

Fig. 5-4: Gluing the strips to a piece of plywood.

Fig. 5-5: Three sections of strips glued on plywood.

Fig. 5-6: Clamping the edges to the plywood.

• Using a table saw or a radial arm saw, cut the backer board so it is 12" square. These strips can be sanded by hand. Don't use a belt or orbital sander. Using an orbital sander, especially, will get the red dust from the blood wood into the grain of the cottonwood and give it a pinkish appearance. You may want to tape off the cottonwood and sand the blood wood and the joint one at a time. Next, make the sides, which can be attached with pocket screws from the back *(Fig. 5-8)*. See "Kreg Pocket Screw Method" in Chapter II.

• See the topic section "Making Eyes" in Chapter II and use the jig saw method. This will explain, in detail, how to make the eyes for the Stern Eagle.

Fig. 5-7: Removing excess glue with a glue scraper.

Fig. 5-8: The sides of the frame.

• Trace the pattern for the left side of the eagle. Trace the eagle's eye *(Fig. 5-9)* and drill a hole through the eye *(Fig. 5-10)*. Insert your jigsaw blade through the hole *(Fig. 5-11)* and cut the eye section out *(Fig. 5-12)*. Glue the eye into the cottonwood in such a way that it is recessed about 1/16" to 1/8" *(Fig. 5-13)*. If the eye sticks out the back of the project, it can be sanded off when it is dry *(Fig. 5-14)*.

• Cut the right side of the eagle's face with a jig saw *(Fig. 5-15)*. Cut the beak out *(Fig. 5-16)*. The right and left side of the face can be put together *(Fig. 5-17)*.

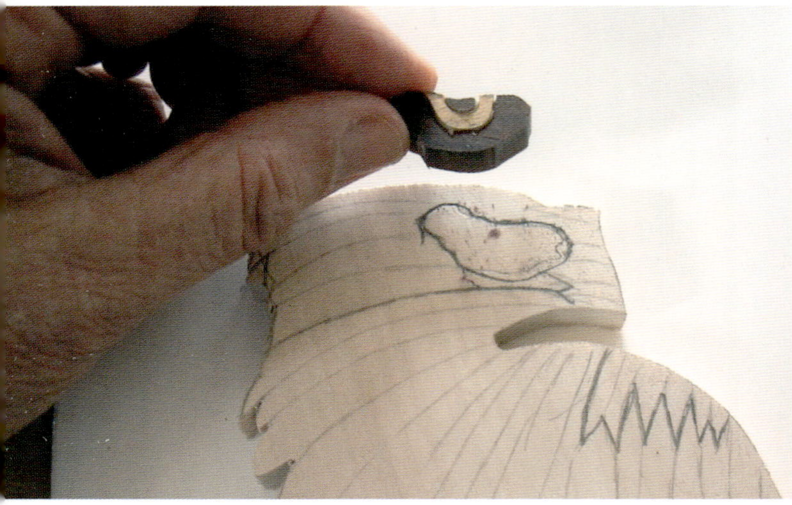

Fig. 5-9: Tracing the eagle's eye.

Fig. 5-10: Drilling a hole for the jig saw blade.

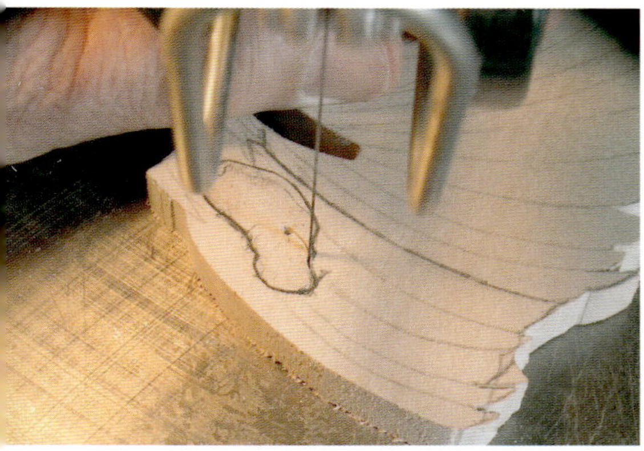

Fig. 5-11: Starting the internal cut.

Fig. 5-12: The eye section has been cut out.

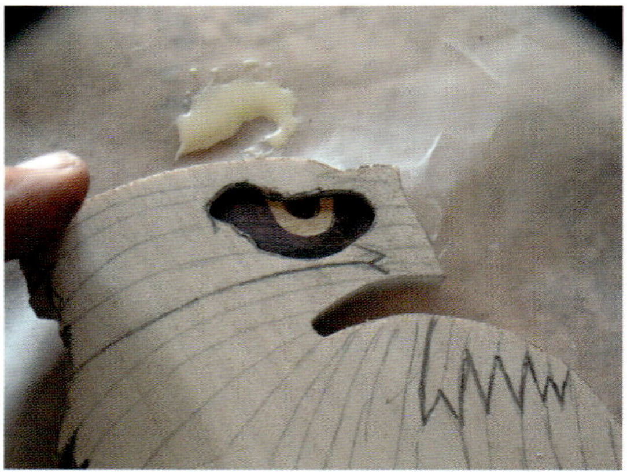

Fig. 5-13: Recess the eye and glue it in.

Fig. 5-14: Once the glue has dried, sand the back flush.

• Now, glue the feathers above the eye and the eye section to a piece of manila folder *(Fig. 5-18)*. Continue gluing the feathers to a manila folder for the right side of the face *(Fig. 5-19)*. Notice the manila folder at the bottom of the photo. Continue this process on the left hand side until the head is finished *(Fig. 5-20)*. Again notice the use of manila folder to keep all the parts together. Look at the pattern and burn the lines in the face using a woodburner.

Fig. 5-15: Cutting the edge of the right side of the face.

Fig. 5-16: Fitting the beak to the right side of the face.

Fig. 5-17: Fitting the right side and left side of the head and the beak together.

Make sure no manila folder shows on the edges of the eagle's face. Then glue the eagle's face to the striped backer board. See "Hangers" in Chapter II for methods of hanging the eagle. I like to use spray lacquer to finish the project.

Fig. 5-18: A section of the right side has been glued to manila paper to keep the parts together.

Fig. 5-19: The assembled right side of the face glued to a piece of manila paper.

Fig. 5-20: The whole face glued to a piece of manila paper, becoming one unit.

Chapter VI

Born Free Eagle

Materials: Parts 1, 2, 28, 29, and 30 are made out of a dark rosewood. The feathers, parts 3 through 14 and parts 17 through 45, are made of wenge. The tail feathers, part 46, can be made of cottonwood or aspen. Parts 47 and 48 are made of wenge and 49 and 50 are made of yellow heart. The mountains and the frame are spalted maple. The white caps on the mountains are aspen or cottonwood. The yellow colored wood for the background is pau amarello. The red stripes in the background as well as the locking pins on the frame are all blood wood.

Refer to Patterns 6-1 to 6-5 for this eagle.

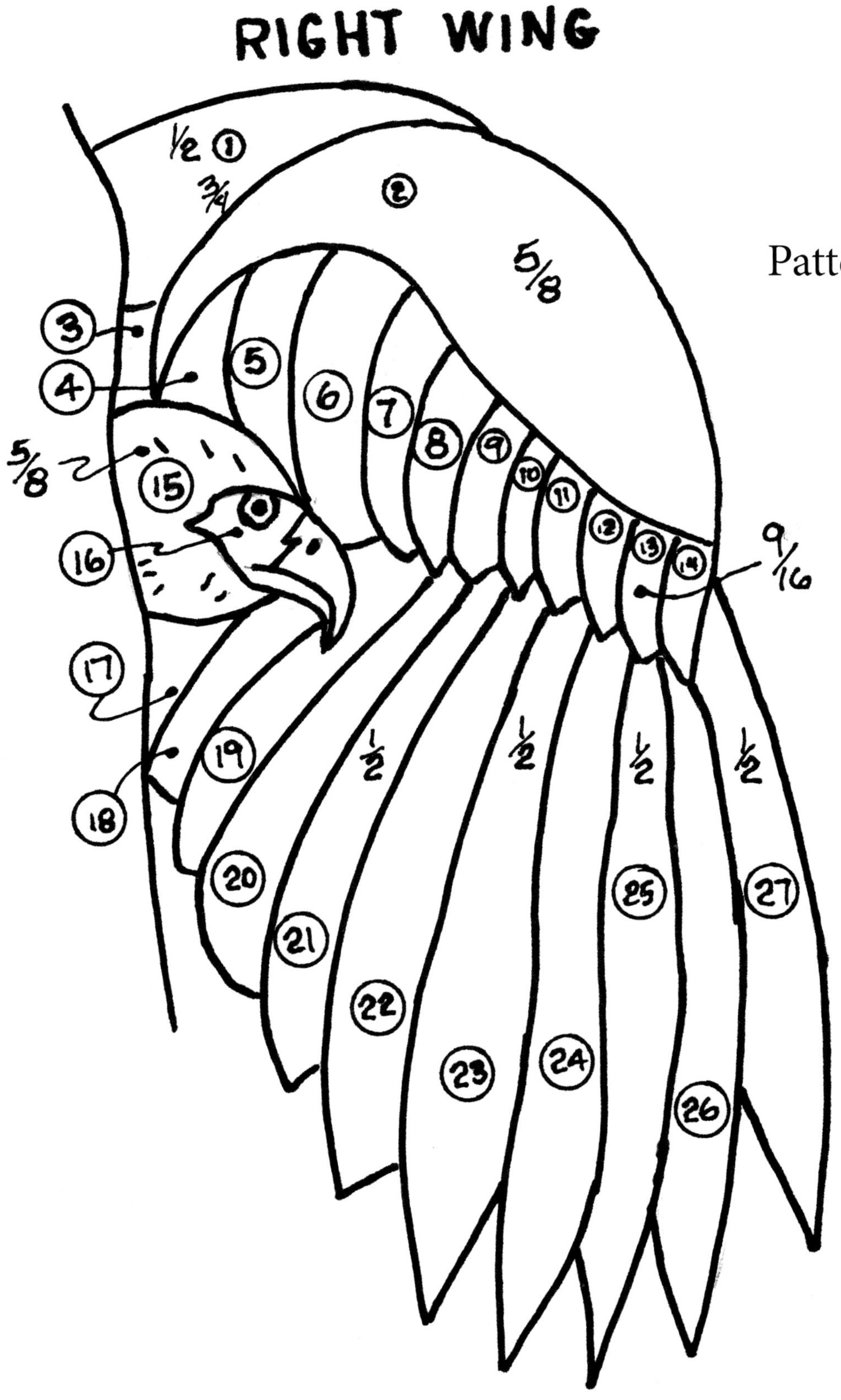

Pattern 6-1

LEFT WING
28
29
30
31
32
33
34
35
36
37
38
39
40
41
42
43
44
45
46
47
48
49
50
3/4
3/4
3/4
5/8
1/2
1/2
1/2
1/2
1/2
1/2
1/2
1/2
1/2
3/8
1/4
1/4
3/16

Pattern 6-2

Pattern 6-3

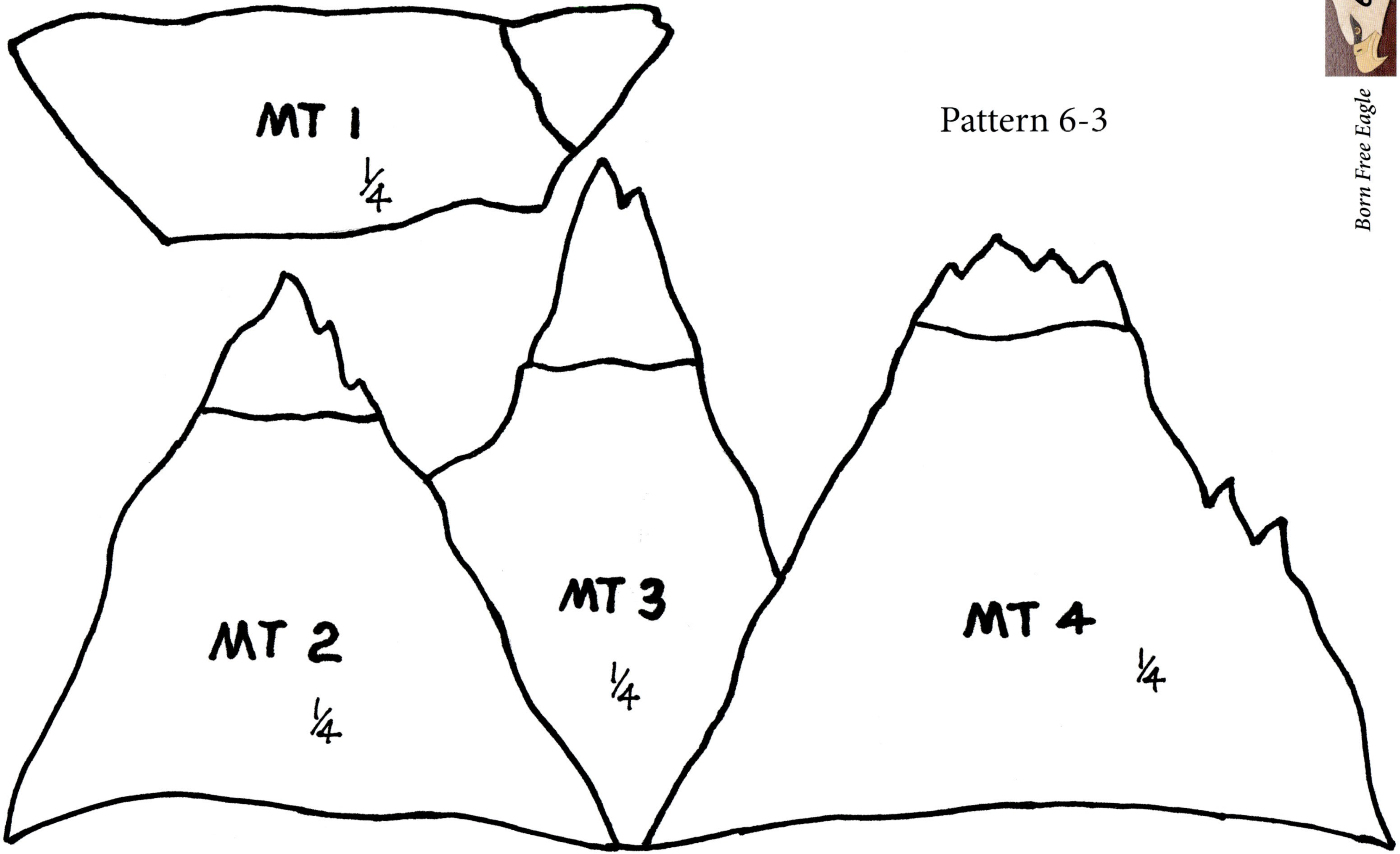

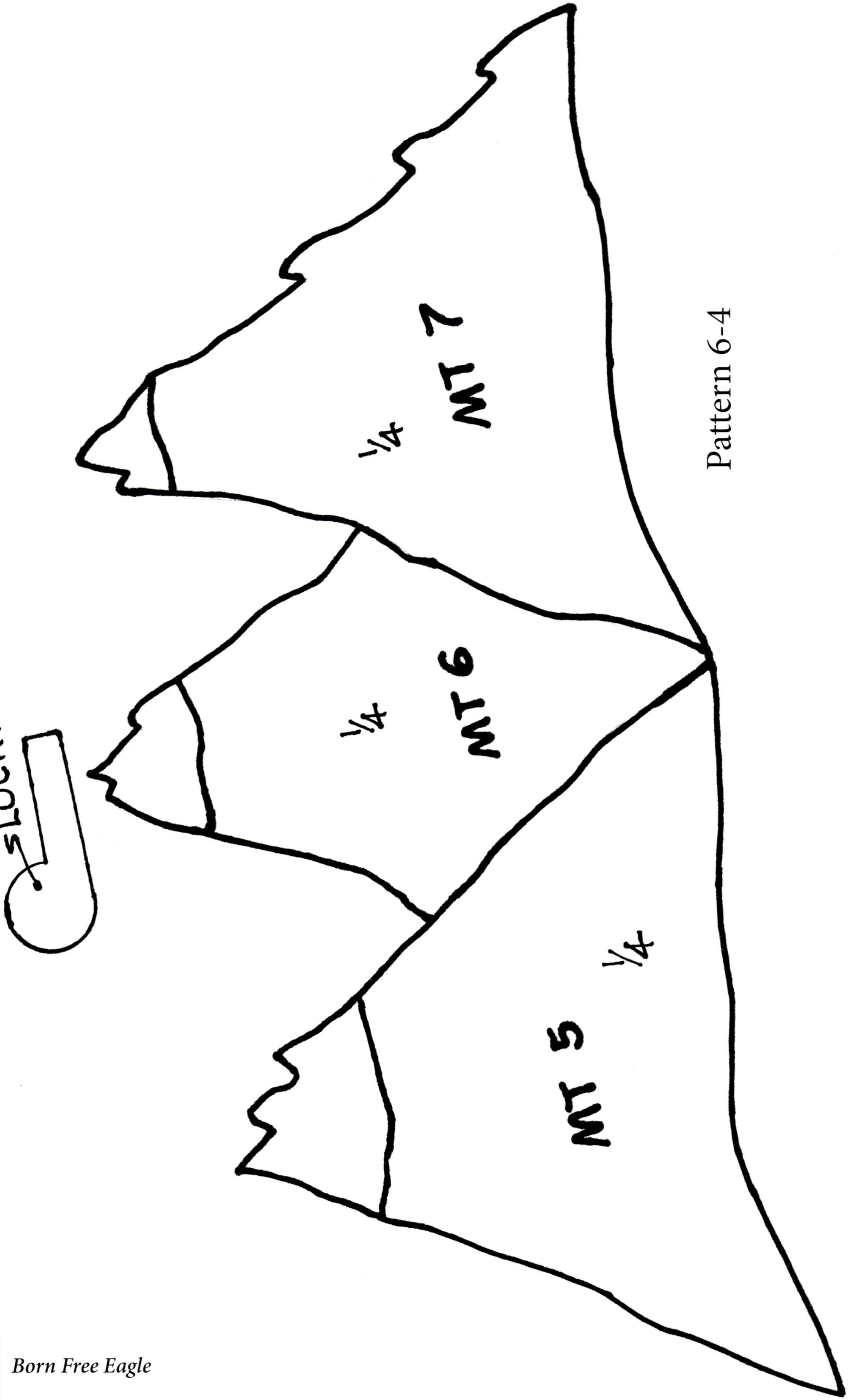

Pattern 6-4

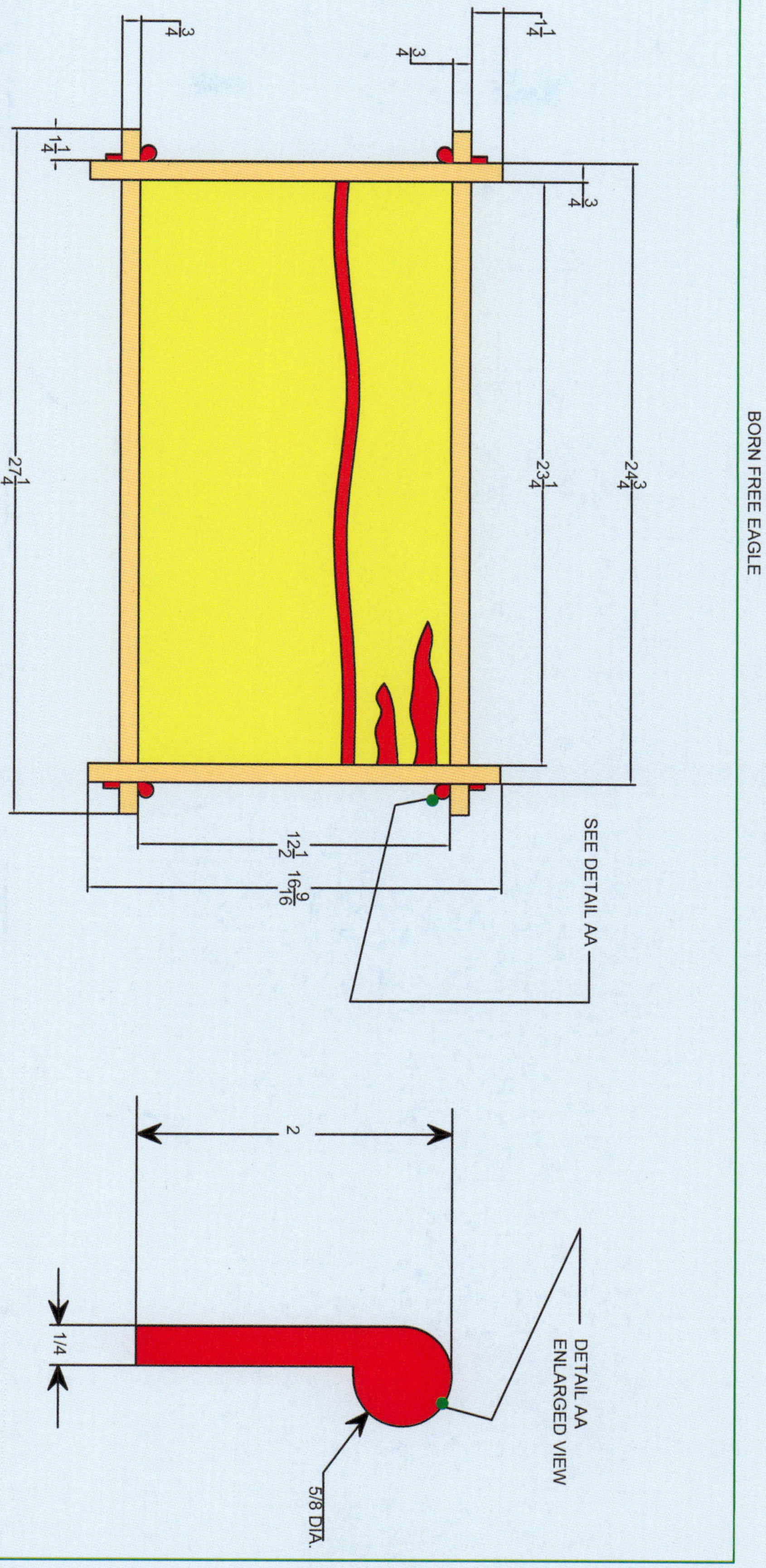

Pattern 6-5: For the frame.

• First cut part 1, then trace part 2 using part 1 to trace the edge where the two parts meet *(Fig. 6-1)*. I cut these out on the band saw. Parts 1 and 2 can be rounded using a disc sander *(Fig. 6-2)*. Use the end of a belt sander or a drum sander to round the inside corners *(Fig. 6-3)*. Do the final sanding using an orbital sander *(Fig. 6-4)* and a Sand-O-Flex.

• Next, cut out parts 4 through 14 as one piece, making sure they fit snuggly against part 2 *(Fig. 6-5)*. In *Fig. 6-6*, parts 4 through 14 are matched with parts 17 through 27; none of the feathers have been cut individually. Be sure the fit is good before proceeding on to the next step. Notice that the head has been cut out which I will use as a pattern on a piece of cottonwood *(Fig. 6-7)*. Cut parts 4 through 14 and 17 through 27 using a jig saw *(Fig. 6-8)*. Round the edges slightly using the end of a belt or a drum sander, about 3/16" radius, then sand these with a Sand-O-Flex sander.

Fig. 6-1: Using part 1 and the pattern to trace part 2.

Fig. 6-3: A belt sander can also be used for rounding edges.

Fig. 6-2: Rounding the edge of part 2 using a disc sander.

Fig. 6-4: Using an orbital sander to produce a finished surface.

Fig. 6-5: Part 1 and 2 fitting against parts 4 through 14.

Fig. 6-6: The wood used for parts 17 through 27 fitting against parts 4 through 14.

Fig. 6-7: Place the wenge head on a piece of cottonwood and trace.

Fig. 6-8: Parts 4 through 27 have been cut out.
The eagle's head is fitted into the feathers.

• Cut out the cottonwood head which was traced from the wenge. Then cut out the beak, part 16, and the eye section *(Fig. 6-9)*. Use the cottonwood beak for the pattern that can be traced on yellow heart *(Fig. 6-10)*. Cut the beak out of the yellow heart and insure a good fit *(Fig. 6-11)*. Then check the fit of the head and the beak inside the feathers *(Fig. 6-12)*.

Fig. 6-12: The finished right wing and the head.

Fig. 6-9: Cutting out part 16, the beak.

Fig. 6-10: Place the beak on a piece of yellow heart and trace.

Fig. 6-11: Fit the yellow heart beak into the cottonwood head.

Fig. 6-13: Use a Forstner bit and a drill press to drill the hole for the eye.

• Use a Forstner bit to drill a 1/4" hole for the eye *(Fig. 6-13)*. See the topic section "Making Eyes" and use the plug cutter method. Glue the eye into the beak and the beak into the head *(Fig. 6-14)*. A Sand-O-Flex sander is a good choice for sanding the head *(Fig. 6-15)*. Use a pair of pliers or vice grips to hold the head. This is much easier than holding it with your fingers and accidently sanding you fingernails thin.

• Again, check the fit for all the parts of the right wing. Glue the right wing to a piece of manila folder *(Fig. 6-16)*, only a very thin amount of glue is needed. I do this to keep all the parts together as one unit. Once these parts are glued together with a paper backing, they stay together nicely. Remove the excess paper from the back around the edges *(Fig. 6-17)*.

Fig. 6-14: Glue the dowel into the yellow heart.

Fig. 6-16: Gluing parts 1 through 14 on a piece of manila folder.

Fig. 6-15: Holding the head with pliers while using the Sand-O-Flex.

Fig. 6-17: The paper has been trimmed on the back of parts 1 through 27.

• Start the left wing next. Notice I used the right wing to trace where the left wing meets parts 28, 29, and 30 *(Fig. 6-18)*. Taper parts 28, 29, and 30 using a band saw. A hand screw clamp is used to hold this since the bottom is not completely flat. This ensures safer operation. Be sure the wing sets on the band saw table as flat as possible. The tapered wing is shown in *Fig. 6-19*. Round the edges with a drum sander and use a Sand-O-Flex sander to finish the wing. Using the same method as on the right wing, cut parts 30 through 45 *(Fig. 6-20)*. Once cut and sanded, glue them to a piece of manila folder, as previously mentioned for the right wing, to make the left wing one unit. Notice I cut out parts 28, 29, and 30 *(Fig. 6-21)*.

Fig. 6-18: Parts 28 through 30 fitted to the right wing.

Fig. 6-19: Parts 28 through 30 as one unit and not yet cut individually.

Fig. 6-20: The feathers for the left wing have been cut out.

Fig. 6-21: The left wing has been glued to a piece of manila folder.

• A woodburner is used for the lines required on parts 15 and 16, the head and the beak *(Fig. 6-22)*.

• Next, cutout the tail feathers using the table jig saw *(Fig. 6-23)*. Be sure the feathers fit correctly *(Fig. 6-24)*.

• Using the same method as above, cut out 47 and 48. Parts 49 and 50 can be cut on a jig saw using yellow heart.

Fig. 6-22: Use a woodburner to burn the lines in the beak.

Fig. 6-23: Cutout the tail feathers on a jig saw.

Fig. 6-24: Checking the fit of the tail feathers.

• To make a backing for the eagle, I use a 1/4" thick red oak or birch plywood. Trace the outside of the left wing *(Fig. 6-25)*, then draw a line inside about 1/4" which will later be the cutting line for the backer board. Do the same for the right wing *(Fig. 6-26)*. Glue the eagle onto the backing *(Fig. 6-27)*. Notice in *Fig. 6-28* I have propped up the claws while they are being glued. Use a black permanent marker to darken the edges of the backing, so when you look at the project from the side you don't notice the white backing. The black blends in better with the eagle's color.

Fig. 6-25: Drawing the outside line of the eagle and the inside line which will be the cutting line for backer board.

Fig. 6-26: The backer board is ready to be cut.

Fig. 6-27: Gluing parts of the eagle to the backer board.

Fig. 6-28: Propping up parts 49 and 50 while they dry.

• Trace and cut out on a table jig saw mountain 1 through mountain 7 *(Fig. 6-29)*. Be sure the mountains fit nicely. The red line in the background is blood wood and represents a sunset over the mountains. Temporarily glue, using CA glue, a piece of 1/4" thick by 3/4" wide blood wood to a piece of pau amarello. Yellow heart would also be a good choice for the background. When I say glue it temporarily, I mean four small spots each, being about 1/4" in diameter. With one piece on top of the other, cut a gently flowing line on both pieces at the same time. Then use a chisel to separate the two pieces using a light tap from the chisel where the glue was applied. These two pieces should fit together exactly. Do the same for the top piece of pau amarello. For the two streaks, use the same process. If you have a problem separating these two, you can sand the yellow heart off on the disc sander. Check the fit and glue. Sand these with a belt sander.

• Occasionally, you may have a crack that did not glue properly. If so, as I did, fill the crack with a sliver of the same color wood *(Fig. 6-30)*. Glue this into the crack. Once dry, sand it smooth with an orbital sander.

• Glue the pau amarello to a sheet of 1/2" plywood for the backing, which shows the mountain and the sky. The frame is made out of 1 1/4" high by 3/4" wide spalted maple, cut to desired length. With the pau amarello already glued to the plywood, glue the two outside frame parts *(Fig. 6-31)*. Once this is dry, trim the end on a radial arm saw or table saw. Glue the end frame parts on so they overlap on each end by exactly 1 1/4" *(Fig. 6-32)*. To make the tenon 3/4" square by 1 1/4", cut a dado in a piece of maple as shown in photo *(Fig. 6-33)*.

Fig. 6-29: Fitting mountains 1 through 7 together.

Fig. 6-31: Using bar clamps to clamp the frame around the backer board.

Fig. 6-30: Sanding a small sliver of wood that has been used to fill a crack.

Fig. 6-32: Clamping the ends of the backer board.

Fig. 6-33: Making a dado cut on the table saw.

When the project is finished, this tenon will appear to run all the way through the vertical boards. Once the dado is cut, rip this board to 3/4" wide by 1 1/4" in length. Cut the red locking pins, blood wood, on a jig saw *(Fig. 6-34)*. If these are not exactly even on the bottom *(Fig. 6-35)*, they can be sanded perfectly flat using a disc sander *(Fig. 6-36)*. Use a 3/8" Forstner bit to drill a hole in the end of this piece about 1" deep *(Fig. 6-37)*. Then use a twist bit *(Fig. 6-38)*, to drill a hole all the way through. This hole will prevent breaking when this piece is attached. Attach this tenon with the round part of the pin as shown, using a Kreg square headed pan screw with fine threads *(Fig. 6-39)*. Once all four tenons are attached, make 3/8" plugs to fill the holes.

• Do any finish touch up, such as sanding the plugs flat. Now your project is ready for a finish *(Fig. 6-40)*. A spray can of lacquer works well. To hang the project on the wall, see "Hanging Methods" in Chapter II.

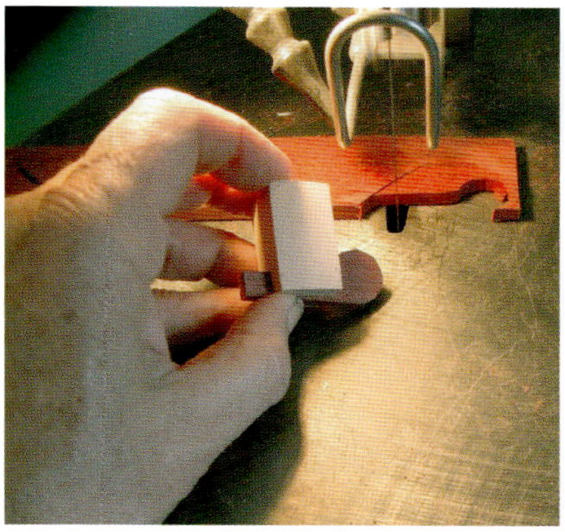

Fig. 6-34: Cutting out the locking pin and checking it's fit.

Fig. 6-38: Use a twist bit to drill a pilot hole for the screws.

Fig. 6-35: Notice that the pin hangs over a little at the bottom.

Fig. 6-39: I like to use Kreg pocket screws to attach the pin.

Fig. 6-36: Sanding the bottom of the locking pin to make it flush.

Fig. 6-40: The complete Born Free Eagle, ready to be finished.

Fig. 6-37: Drilling a countersink hole using a Forstner bit and a drill press.

Chapter VII

The Great Seal of the United States of America

Materials: The shield, part 1, has two parts: the red and white stripes, which are made of cottonwood and blood wood, and the blue section, which is a piece of cottonwood stained blue. General Finishes® makes the blue, water-based dye stain. I used two coats to get a dark blue result. The olive branches, part 2, are made of lignum vitae. The feet, part 3, are made of yellow heart; the tail feathers, part 4 and 10, are made of cottonwood; and part 5 and 6, the wings and legs, are made of walnut. Part 7 is a piece of cottonwood stained blue. Part 8 is cottonwood stained yellow. Part 9 is cottonwood stained blue. The round disc is made of cottonwood and the three stripes around the outside of the disc is made of walnut.

Refer to *Patterns 7-1 to 7-3* for this eagle.

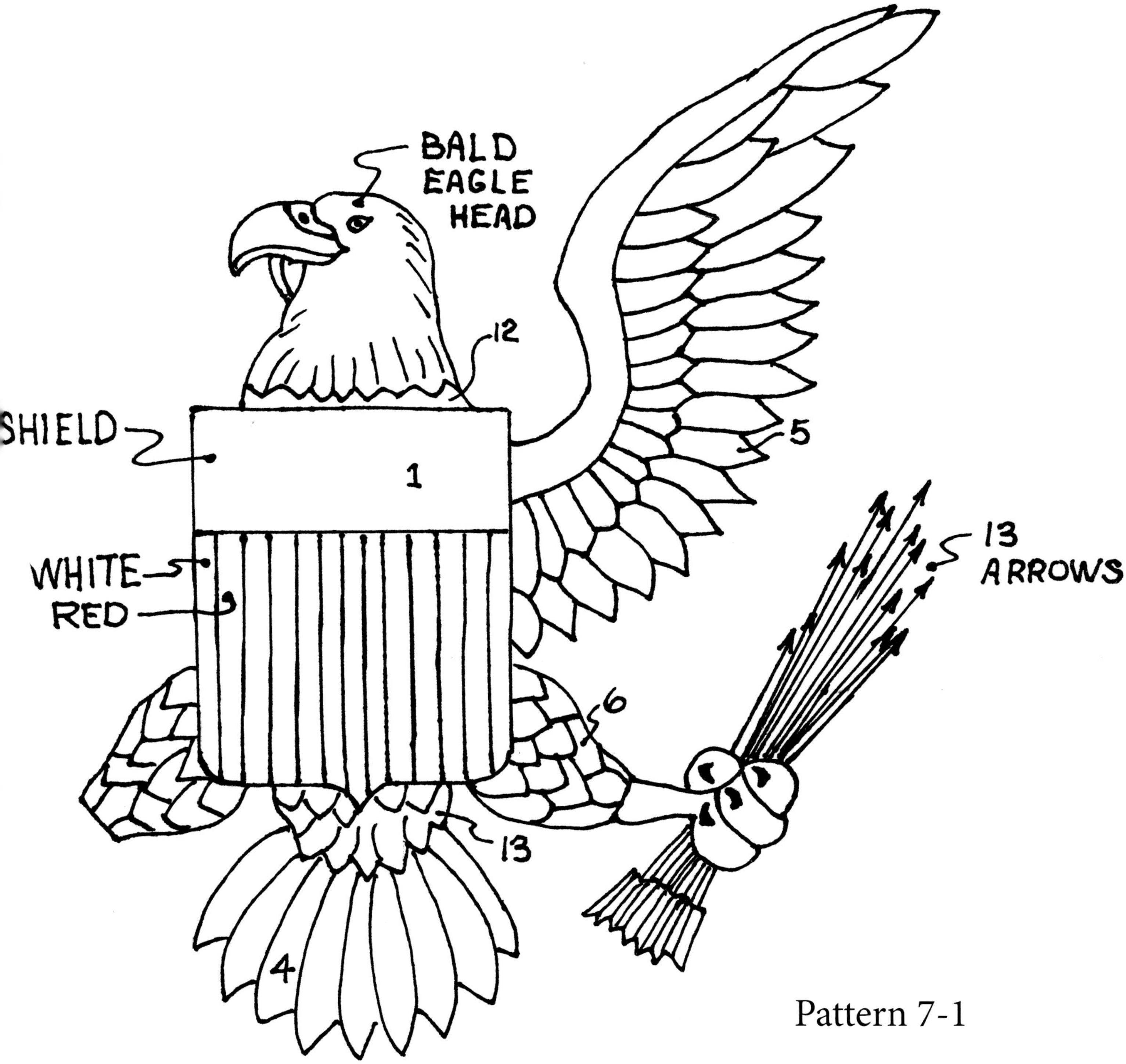

Pattern 7-1

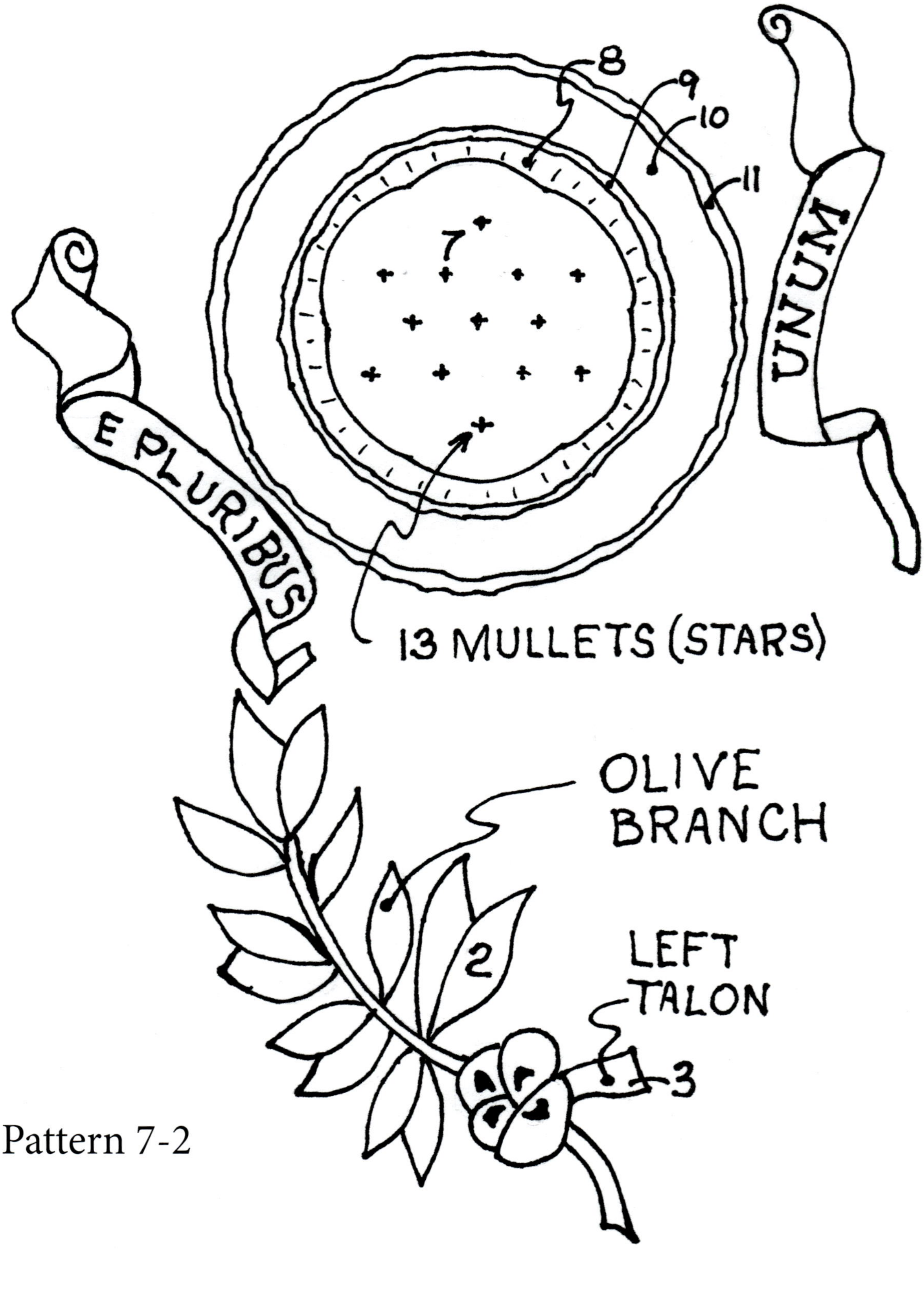
8
9
10
11
7
UNUM
E PLURIBUS
13 MULLETS (STARS)
OLIVE
BRANCH
2
LEFT
TALON
3

Pattern 7-2

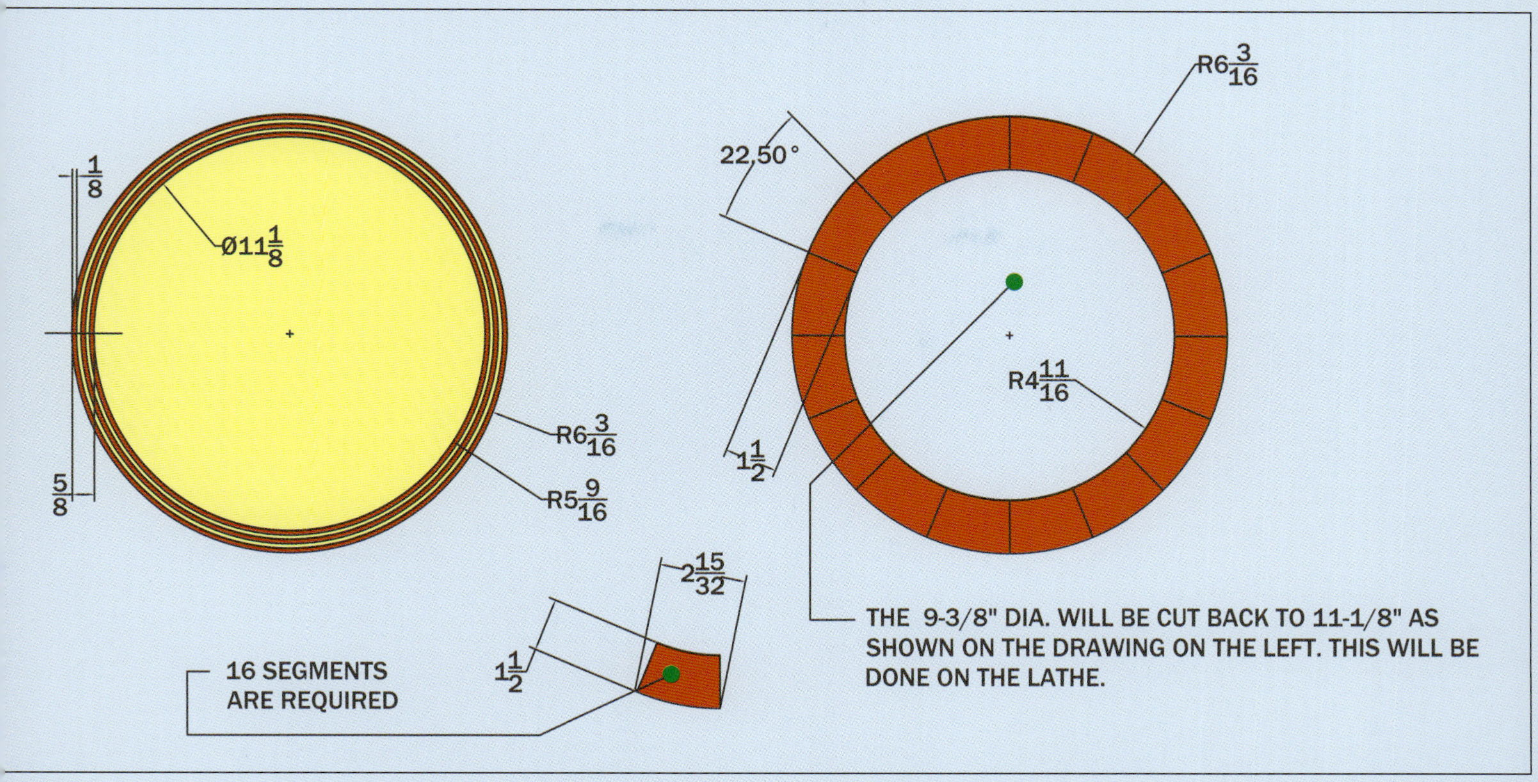

Pattern 7-3

• To start the shield, part 1, cut 13 segments from a practice board. I use a less expensive piece of wood for the practice. The objective is to have 13 pieces that are 2 1/4" wide. *Figure 7-1* shows that the 13 pieces are 3" wide. Rip another piece that is slightly skinnier than the previous piece. Cut this piece into 13 segments and check to see if it is 2 1/4" wide. *Figure 7-2* shows that it is 2 7/16" wide. On the third try, I got this right, exactly 2 1/4" when they are clamped *(Fig. 7-3)*.

Fig. 7-2: A second practice, still not correct; it should be 2 1/4".

Fig 7-1: Cutting practice strips for the eagle's shield.

Fig. 7-3: After three tries, I got the strips to be exactly 2 1/4".

• Without changing the fence on the table saw, rip enough blood wood and cottonwood to make the red and white stripes for part 1, the shield *(Fig. 7-4)*. Make sure the cottonwood is on the outside on each side. Be sure the 2 1/4" measurement is correct *(Fig. 7-5)*. Glue these 13 pieces together *(Fig. 7-6)*. Flatten one side on the belt sander *(Fig. 7-7)*. *Figure 7-8* shows cutting the striped section to the correct thickness, which is 1/2". Use the pattern and cut the striped section out as well as the blue section of the shield, part 1.

Fig. 7-6: Use wax paper when clamping to keep your vice, clamp, and floor clean.

Fig. 7-4: Cutting the blood wood strips on the table saw.

Fig. 7-7: Sanding one edge flat using a disc sander.

Fig. 7-5: Making sure the strips are the correct size.

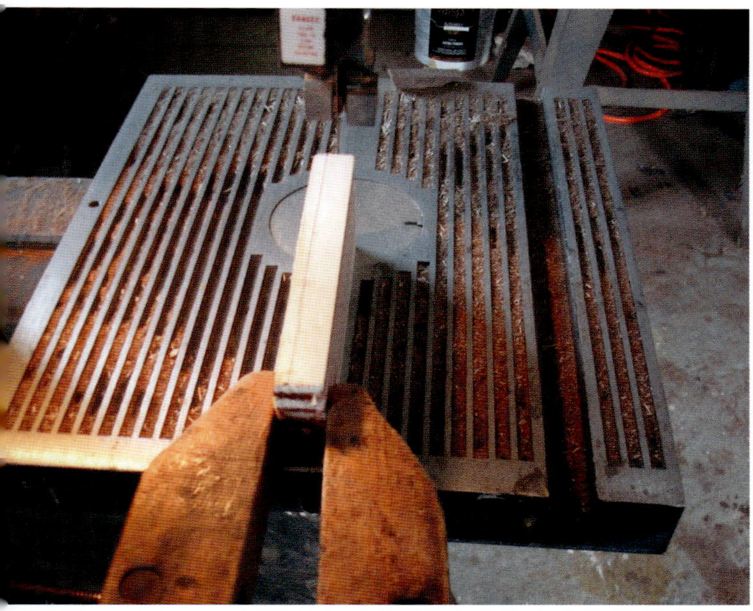

Fig. 7-8: Using a band saw to cut the striped strips to the correct thickness.

Fig. 7-10: Flatten the edge that fits against the shield using a disc sander.

• Start part 5, the wings, by tracing the pattern on a piece of walnut. The walnut should be 1/4" thick *(Fig. 7-9)*. Both the right and the left wing are the same pattern but one is a mirror image of the other, so make two wings. Sand the side that fits against the shield flat to ensure a nice straight surface *(Fig. 7-10)*. Trace the wings and draw all the feathers as shown *(Fig. 7-11)*.

Fig. 7-9: Trace both wings, part 5.

Fig. 7-11: The wing is ready to be cut out.

• Cut these out on a table jig saw *(Fig. 7-12)*. Use a woodburner to burn the lines on the wings as shown in *Fig. 7-13*. Use a flip sander to sand the wings after you have finished burning all the feathers in *(Fig. 7-14)*. Round the edges slightly. *Figure 7-15* shows the two finished wings.

Fig. 7-12: Cutting the outside of the feathers.

Fig. 7-14: Sand the right and left wing using a Sand-O-Flex sander.

Fig. 7-13: Use a woodburner to outline the feathers.

Fig. 7-15: The finished wings.

• The head of the eagle and the beak can be made next by cutting a notch or a rabbit joint on the end of a piece of 1/2" thick cottonwood *(Fig. 7-16)*. Out of a piece of walnut, cut out part 12 so it will fit under the head as shown *(Fig. 7-17)*. The head and part 12 are shown here *(Fig. 7-18)*. Next, cut out the beak as shown *(Fig. 7-19)*. Trace this beak on a piece of 1/2" thick yellow heart *(Fig. 7-20)*.

Fig. 7-18: The back of the head and part 12. They are not quite flush, but that's okay.

Fig. 7-16: A rabbit joint cut into the piece of cottonwood used for the head.

Fig. 7-19: Cut the beak out of the cottonwood.

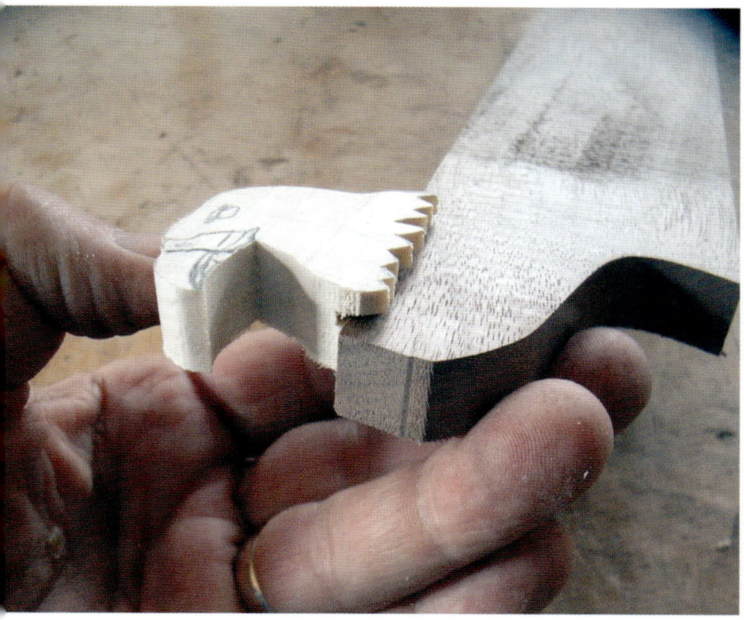

Fig. 7-17: Be sure the head fits over part 12 and both are flush on the back.

Fig. 7-20: The cottonwood beak has been used to trace the pattern on the yellow heart.

• Cut the beak out so it will fit nicely into the head *(Fig. 7-21)*. Glue these two parts together. Remove any excess glue with a sharp knife *(Fig. 7-22)*. Cut part 1 out of a piece of cottonwood. *Figure 7-23* shows all the parts made to this point. You may notice that I have not stained the top part of the shield, which is deep blue.

Fig. 7-21: This is an acceptable fit.

Fig. 7-22: Removing any excess glue.

Fig. 7-23: This photo shows all the parts you made thus far, including part 1.

• Start parts 7 through 11 by cutting the outside shape of part 11 from a piece of cottonwood which is about 3/8" thick *(Fig. 7-24)*. Part 7 through 11 are all made out of this one piece. Next, drill holes as shown in *Fig. 7-25* so these parts can be separated. Cut part 11 out by inserting your blade through the hole and finish cutting part 11 *(Figs. 7-26 & 7-27)*. Make a straight line across the back as shown *(Fig. 7-28)*.

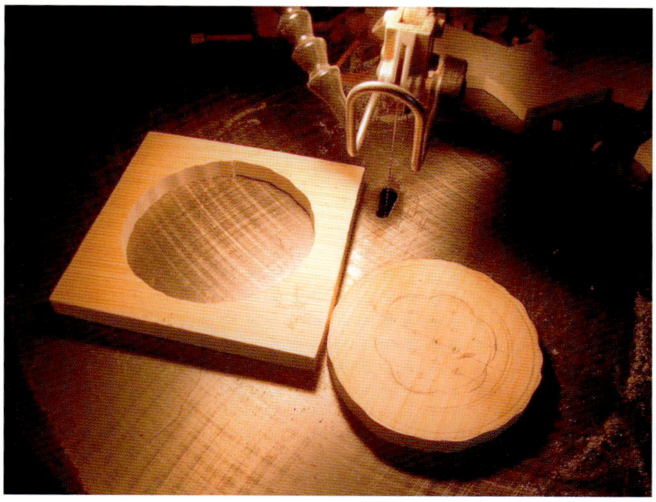

Fig. 7-24: The outside of part 11 has been cut out.

Fig. 7-25: Holes drilled to insert the jig saw blade.

Fig. 7-26: The jig saw blade inserted into the cottonwood.

Fig. 7-27: Starting an internal cut.

Fig. 7-28: A pencil mark on the back of parts 7 through 11 will help to realign the parts since the cut line is circular. This cut would be hard to realign without the pencil mark reference.

This helps to line these parts up later after they have been stained. On part 7, lay out the positions for the thirteen mullets, the stars *(Fig. 7-29)*. Cut out parts 7 through 11. Stain part 10 yellow *(Fig. 7-30)*. Also, stain parts 11, 9, and 7 blue. Now, stain the blue part of the shield, part 1. Drill the holes in part 7 *(Fig. 7-31)*. These are for the mullets, the stars, to fit into. After these parts are stained, glue these together *(Figs. 7-32 & Fig. 7-33)*. See "Resources for Materials" in Chapter II to find a vendor for the stars. Use a drop of clear thick CA glue and glue the stars into the holes *(Fig. 7-34)*.

Fig. 7-29: Use an awl to mark the points to drill for the mullets (stars).

Fig. 7-30: Part 8 has been stained yellow.

Fig. 7-31: After staining parts 11, 9, 7, and 1, drill the holes in part 7.

Fig. 7-32: Gluing part 9 to part 8.

Fig. 7-33: Gluing part 10 to its adjoining parts.

Fig. 7-34: Using thick, clear CA glue to glue the mullets (stars).

• The round back disc can be made by gluing enough cottonwood so you have a disc that is 13" in diameter *(Fig. 7-35)*. Once dry, use a glue scraper to remove the excess glue *(Fig. 7-36)*. Sand one side only with a belt sander, this will become the back of the project *(Fig. 7-37)*. Using a long compass, see "Compass" in Chapter II, or tramble points, draw a 13" circle *(Fig. 7-38)*.

Fig. 7-36: Removing dried glue with a glue scraper.

Fig. 7-35: Gluing up two pieces of cottonwood for the backer board.

Fig. 7-37: Use a belt sander to sand the backer board.

Fig. 7-38: Drawing a circle for the backer board using a compass.

Be sure to mark the center *(Fig. 7-39)*. Cut the round disc out on the band saw as shown in *Fig. 7-40*. On the side that you sanded, attach a faceplate as shown in *Fig. 7-41*. The center that you previously marked should be approximately in the center of the faceplate. Screw the faceplate on the disc.

Fig. 7-39: Be sure to mark the center of the backer board.

Fig. 7-40: Cutting the backer board out on the band saw.

Fig. 7-41: Screwing a backer board to a faceplate.

• To make the outside ring, which is made of walnut, I use a process called segmented turning. See "Segmented Turning" in Chapter II. Cut out 16 segments; I like to use a power miter box *(Fig. 7-42)*. On a piece of wax paper, lay these segments out *(Fig. 7-43)*. Clamp all 16 segments together without glue to make sure they fit correctly *(Fig. 7-44)*. See the Pattern 7-3 for the exact size of the segments. Once you see that your ring fits correctly, glue the segments together making sure you have glue on both sides of each segment *(Fig. 7-45)*. Notice the direction of the grain. You will be gluing end grain as you go around the ring. *Figure 7-46* shows the ring on a piece of wax paper, which keeps the table somewhat clean. I use an electric drill to tighten the hose clamp *(Fig. 7-47)*. Once this is dry, screw it to a plywood disc which is mounted on a faceplate and then put it on the lathe. Notice I have countersunk all the screws by about 1/4". Use a diamond-nosed tool to flatten the walnut ring *(Fig. 7-48)*. Use a parting tool to cut straight in, making the outside of the ring perfectly round *(Fig. 7-49)*.

Fig. 7-45: Glue both edges of each segment.

Fig. 7-46: Glue the segmented ring using a hose clamp.

Fig. 7-47: I like to use an electric drill to tighten the hose clamp.

Fig. 7-42: Cutting the walnut segments.

Fig. 7-43: Several of the walnut segments positioned into a semi-circle.

Fig. 7-48: The walnut ring attached to a scrap board. Here, it is being flattened with a diamond-nosed tool.

Fig. 7-44: Be sure the sixteen segments fit with precision before continuing.

Fig. 7-49: The outside can be made round by cutting straight in with a parting tool.

• Next, put the cottonwood disc on the lathe and flatten it as shown *(Fig. 7-50)*. With the walnut ring and the disc flat, glue these two flat surfaces together as shown *(Fig. 7-51)*. Cut away the walnut ring so it is only 3/4" wide *(Fig. 7-52)* and about 3/16" thick. Then cut the two grooves as shown *(Fig. 7-53)* using a parting tool.

Fig. 7-50: After the cottonwood disc has been turned flat, check it with a straight edge, like the board shown.

Fig. 7-51: Clamping and gluing the walnut ring to the cottonwood backer board.

Fig. 7-52: Use a diamond-nosed tool to flatten the walnut as well as the cottonwood.

Fig. 7-53: Using a parting tool to cut the groove in the walnut.

Figure 7-54 shows the cut all the way down to the cottonwood, where you should stop cutting. *Figure 7-55* shows most of the walnut being cut away but not all. Check to be sure all the walnut has been removed. *Figure 7-56* shows the finished disc. Cut a contour or a curve to your liking on the edge *(Fig. 7-57)*. I usually use a round-nosed lathe tool for this as shown in *Fig. 7-58*. Sand the disc *(Fig. 7-59)*.

Fig. 7-54: The two grooves cut with the parting tool.

Fig. 7-55: Check and be sure there is no walnut left in the groove, as there is in this photo.

Fig. 7-56: The finished backer board.

Fig. 7-57: The edge has been rounded to a rough state.

Fig. 7-58: I use a round-nosed tool to cut a molding type cut in the edge.

Fig. 7-59: Sanding the disc as it turns.

• Trace part 13 and make sure it fits correctly with the shield. It should be the same thickness as the shield. Cut out part 13 on the jig saw *(Figs. 7-60 & 7-61)*. Next, trace the bottom section of part 13 on a piece of cottonwood *(Fig. 7-62)*. Then, finish tracing the feathers, part 4 *(Fig. 7-63)*. Again, use a jig saw to cut this out *(Fig. 7-64)*.

Fig. 7-60: Fitting the striped section of the shield into part 13.

Fig. 7-63: Part 4 is ready to be cut.

Fig. 7-61: Using a jig saw to cut out part 13.

Fig. 7-62: Trace the bottom of part 13 onto a piece of cottonwood, then trace the pattern for part 4, the tail feathers.

Fig. 7-64: First cut the top section of part 4.

Notice that part 4 is only about 1/4" thick. Check the fit between part 4 and part 13 *(Fig. 7-65)*. Cut part 6, the legs, using the same process as in part 13. Once it fits nicely, draw or trace the feathers on part 4 *(Fig. 7-66)*. Cut these feathers out using a thin jig saw blade *(Fig. 7-67)*. All of these parts can now be sanded. I hold the small parts with a pair pliers and sand them on the Sand-O-Flex sander *(Fig. 7-68)*. Parts 13 and 4 are glued together on a piece of manila folder, which makes it easier to keep all the parts together as one unit *(Figs. 7-69 & 7-70)*. Once this is dry, I can cut the paper away and these will stay together as one piece.

• Trace the thirteen arrows on a piece of cottonwood *(Fig. 7-71)* and burn them with a woodburner *(Fig. 7-72)*. Then, cut out the left and right legs and talons from a piece of yellow heart. Cut around the arrows as shown *(Fig. 7-73)*, making sure they fit correctly on the right leg and talon.

Fig. 7-65: Check the fit between part 13 and part 4.

Fig. 7-66: Part 6 fits against the shield and part 4 is ready to be cut.

Fig. 7-67: Part 4 after it has been cut.

Fig. 7-68: Hold the tail feathers, part 4, with a pair of pliers and sand with a Sand-O-Flex sander.

Fig. 7-69: Spread out some glue on a manila folder to glue part 13 and part 4 together.

Fig. 7-70: Gluing part 13 and part 4.

Fig. 7-71: Make sure you have 13 arrows and draw these on a piece of cottonwood.

Fig. 7-72: Burning the arrows using a woodburner.

Fig. 7-73: The arrows fitting into part 3.

• To make the olive branch, I use lignum vitae. Start by cutting out the stem *(Fig. 7-74)*, then cut out the leaves *(Fig. 7-75)*. Place these leaves against the stem to be sure they look correct *(Fig. 7-76)*. Hold these with a pair of pliers and sand them on a Sand-O-Flex sander. *Figure 7-77* shows the completed olive branch. Mark the feathers on part 6 and part 3 as well as the talons *(Fig. 7-78)*. These can be burnt in with a woodburner.

Fig. 7-74: The stem for the olive branch is made of lignum vitae.

Fig. 7-77: The olive branch and stem have been sanded.

Fig. 7-75: Tracing the leaves of the olive branch.

Fig. 7-78: Trace the feathers on part 6 and draw the lines on part 3.

Fig. 7-76: Placing the leaves on the stem.

• *Figure 7-79* shows the progress thus far. Layout all the eagle parts on the backer board. Start gluing them on individually with titebond glue *(Fig. 7-80)*. *Figure 7-81* shows all the parts glued on the backer board.

Fig. 7-79: Place the eagle on the backer board and mark the location of the various parts.

Fig. 7-80: Gluing on the shield using titebond glue.

Fig. 7-81: All the parts made thus far glued onto the backer board.

• Now we will make the olives (little circles). Start by cutting a piece of lignum vitae to 3 to 6" long and 3/4" square *(Fig. 7-82)*. Next, cut the end *(Fig. 7-83)*. This is so the drive center will fit into the grooves easier. Put this on a lathe, between the drive center and the dead center *(Fig. 7-84)*. Use a gouge to get this round *(Fig. 7-85)*. Use a diamond-nosed tool to cut the lignum vitae down to 1/4" diameter *(Fig. 7-86)*. Notice I have left the ends square *(Fig. 7-87)*. Sand this while it is on the lathe. Then, cut the square ends off on the jig saw *(Fig. 7-88)*. Lay a piece of plywood on the table of your jig saw so the olives will not fall through the throat of the jig saw. Cut the olives to about 1/16" thickness *(Fig. 7-89)*.

Fig. 7-82: Mark an X on the end of a piece of lignum vitae, which will be used for the olives.

Fig. 7-83: Cut on one end as shown. This is where the drive center should go.

Fig. 7-84: Mount the lignum vitae on the lathe between centers.

Fig. 7-85: Use a small gouge to cut the square piece round.

Fig. 7-86: Use a diamond-nosed tool to cut this to about 1/4" diameter.

Fig. 7-87: Notice that both ends are left square.

Fig. 7-88: Cut the square ends off using a jig saw.

Fig. 7-89: Cut the olive to about 1/16" thick using a jig saw. Notice the plywood underneath to keep the olives from falling through the throat of the jig saw table.

• On a piece of cottonwood, draw the two banners *(Fig. 7-90)* and cut one banner out using the jig saw. Continue to cut out the second banner *(Fig. 7-91)*. Use a woodburner to darken the edges *(Fig. 7-92)* and burn the letters in. For these small parts *(Fig. 7-93)* I use a thick, clear CA glue to attach them to the cottonwood disc.

• *Figure 7-94* shows the completed project.

• See "Hangers" in Chapter II for hanging the eagle. For finishing, I like to use a can of spray lacquer.

Fig. 7-90: This banner has been cutout on the jig saw.

Fig. 7-92: Use a woodburner to darken the edges of the banner as well as the lettering.

Fig. 7-91: Cutting the second banner.

Fig. 7-93: I use a thick, clear CA glue to glue on small parts. I like to use a knife to move the small parts around without disturbing the other parts.

Fig. 7-94: The finished great seal is ready to be finished with lacquer.